WOODY ALLEN

CASEBOOKS ON MODERN DRAMATISTS
KIMBALL KING, *General Editor*

Woody Allen
A Casebook

EDITED BY
KIMBALL KING

ROUTLEDGE
NEW YORK LONDON
2001

Published in 2001 by
Routledge
29 West 35th Street
New York, NY 10001

Published in Great Britain by
Routledge
11 New Fetter Lane
London EC4P 4EE

Routledge is an imprint of the Taylor & Francis Group.

10 9 8 7 6 5 4 3 2 1

Printed on acid-free, 250-year-life paper
Manufactured in the United States of America

Library of Congress Cataloging-in-Publication Data

Woody Allen : a casebook / edited by Kimball King.
    p. cm. — (Garland reference library of the humanities ; . v. 2092. Casebooks on
  modern dramatists ; v. 29)
  Includes bibliographical references.
  ISBN 0-8153-3124-X
    1. Allen, Woody—Criticism and interpretation. I. King, Kimball. II. Garland reference
library of the humanities ; vol. 2092. III. Garland reference library of the humanities.
Casebooks on modern dramatists ; . vol. 29.
PN1998.3.A45 W66 2001
791.43'092—dc21

00-065303

Contents

General Editor's Note

KIMBALL KING

Woody Allen, who first became famous as a stand-up comedian and writer of comedy routines, also has had a distinguished career as a playwright, actor, and screenwriter/director. While his celebrity status may be attributed to some of his better-known, early films, such as *Annie Hall, Manhattan, Hannah and Her Sisters* and *Crimes and Misdemeanors,* he has produced more than ten new films in the past decade. This Casebook discusses one of Allen's earliest stage plays, *Don't Drink the Water*, in the context of his theater work, but quickly moves on to his cinematic achievements. While many of his classic films from the 1970s or 1980s are discussed in this volume, special emphasis has been given to his more recent work that is not included in the many critical books that focus on Allen's contributions to American culture. This Casebook attempts to celebrate the depth, complexity, and charm of one of the country's most independent creative artists.

Introduction

KIMBALL KING

I believe that nearly every intelligent person has a favorite Woody Allen film. Whether he or she is a Shakespearean scholar or a contractor or a salesperson, anyone can recall individual scenes, musical scores, or particular acting performances that have provided comforting diversions as well as stimulating thought. In *Woody Allen: A Casebook* I asked several authors of full-length books on Woody Allen as well as theater scholars, musicians, graduate students, and dramaturgs which of Allen's works they wished to comment on. The result is a mixture of essays that capture the invigorating spirit of a great writer, actor, and director. The first three essays in the text cover general topics applicable to most Woody Allen films. Next, Woody Allen's first full-length work for the stage is discussed in detail, *Don't Drink the Water* (1966), as is its adaptation for television a few years later. Allen's *Manhattan* (1979) and *Crimes and Misdemeanors* (1989) are, of course, inexhaustible subjects and they are analyzed here from new perspectives. Finally, later Allen works are discussed in some detail: *The Purple Rose of Cairo* (1985), *Alice* (1989), *Deconstructing Harry* (1997), *Celebrity* (1998), *Everyone Says I Love You* (1995) and *Sweet and Lowdown* (1999), all of which attest to Allen's continuing inventiveness and perspicacity. Finally, a friend and biographer of the artist offers his reflections on personal conversations with Allen over the years. The result is a range of formal and informal critical approaches to the study of an enigmatic and endlessly fascinating chronicler of American life in the last half of the twentieth century, and hopefully a foundation for evaluating works by the talented Woody Allen for years to come.

Carol Goodson's essay, "The Song as Subtext," draws attention to the primacy of musical background in Allen's films. Interestingly, Goodson is a librarian at the State University of West Georgia. She has given readings at the Film and Literature Conference at Florida State University. She is a founding editor of the *Electronic Journal of Library Science for Distance Education*. Her essay, inspired by her master's thesis, shows how films as different as *Radio Days* (1997) and *Hannah and Her Sisters* (1986) are enriched by musical scores which emphasize their major content and themes.

Similarly, Sage Hamilton Rountree speaks in more general terms about Allen's filmic conventions. In particular she is interested in the metanarrative elements and self-reflexive techniques in Allen's work that place him in a postmodernist context. Her doctoral dissertation, similarly, analyzes the treatment, by playwrights, of the professor/protagonist in modern plays, which often involves a self-conscious hero or heroine, capable of contextualizing his or her own presence in the playwright's narrative.

Next, Marie-Phoenix Rivet, a French scholar who was pursuing her studies in American libraries while this book was being assembled, has selected elements from her ongoing investigation of the Persona in Woody Allen's works, to describe the persona's major attributes, its origin in Jewish culture, and its self-referential quality. Particularly helpful to Rivet's assessment are the commentaries from French film critics in periodicals such as the famous *Cahiers du Cinéma*.

The first three critics in this text were introduced to Woody Allen in movies. So it is particularly interesting when William Hutchings, a professor at the University of Alabama at Birmingham, evaluates Allen as a writer for the stage. Although Allen has written *Don't Drink the Water* (1966), *Play It Again, Sam* (1968), and *The Floating Light Bulb* (1981), as well as some one-act plays, he evidently decided at some point that his gifts were more suited to the screen. Hutchings reveals the strengths of Allen's contribution to both media in his discussion of the Broadway and television versions of *Don't Drink the Water*. Hutchings is well qualified to probe Allen's methodology, having assembled his own casebook on David Storey for the present series, and having contributed essays to many other volumes in Garland's two modern drama series. He is also the author of *The Plays of David Storey: A Thematic Study* (1988), a classic of contemporary dramatic criticism. While *Don't Drink the Water* is an early, and perhaps inchoate, example of the author's talents, Allen's *Manhattan* established him as a filmmaker of international renown and presented audiences with a more meaningful screenplay than they were accustomed to seeing.

Lee Fallon, who is completing his doctorate at the University of North Carolina, has written of allegorical and spiritual elements in *Manhattan* that have been overlooked by previous critics, in an essay which alludes to the "Fisher King" myth as it has been used by T. S. Eliot, James Frazer, and Jessie Weston.

Following *Manhattan* by ten years, *Crimes and Misdemeanors* is one of Allen's most frequently discussed films. Appropriately, Sander Lee is best known for *Woody Allen's Angst: Philosophical Commentaries in his Serious Films* (1990). In this instance he explores existential issues in *Crimes and Misdemeanors* and other important Allen films, concluding that Allen is well versed in mainstream philosophy and consciously appropriating metaphysical concepts and ethical dilemmas in his works.

Approaching *Crimes and Misdemeanors* from a musical, rather than a philosophical perspective, Thomas Fahy, a concert pianist who is also writing a doctoral dissertation in the American Studies Division of the University of North Carolina's English Department, indicates the extent to which Allen's musical selections for his film illustrate and intensify his social message and furthermore delineate the status of his principal characters.

Moving to later films, we see that William Hutchings, already introduced to the Casebook reader when I cited his essay on *Don't Drink the Water,* is especially drawn to Allen's *The Purple Rose of Cairo.* In "Some of Us Are Real, Some Are Not," Hutchings elucidates Americans' love of movies and explains the fantasies they attempt to fulfill.

Fantasies, of course, are the subject matter of Allen's movie, *Alice,* and playwright Ayckbourn's *Woman in Mind,* as Karen Blansfield points out. Blansfield is a professor and dramaturg in the Dramatic Arts Department at the University of North Carolina. She has written a book on O. Henry and is compiling a research guide to the works of Michael Frayn. Her doctoral dissertation on Frayn began as a survey of the major dramatists of English middle-class life: Alan Ayckbourn, Peter Nichols, and Michael Frayn. In the present essay she makes a dazzling comparison between the frustrations, triumphs, and defeats of an Ayckbourn character, Susan, in *Woman in Mind* and the enigmatic Alice in Allen's movie *Alice.* Her study reveals much about the place of women in contemporary society and in the structure of Allen's movies.

Because the character Alice appears at times to hint at elements in the personal life of the actress who played her, Mia Farrow, *Deconstructing Harry* led to speculation that Allen was revealing his own psyche on screen. No less than three essays in this volume concentrate on this particular film, which has in fact inspired a film symposium (see bibliography). First, Gaylord Brewer contextualizes *Deconstructing Harry* in a series of films that define the 1990s. Brewer is an associate professor at Middle Tennessee State University, where he founded and edits *Poems & Plays*. His criticism includes *David Mamet and Film* (1993) and articles in *Contemporary Literature, American Drama,* and *Literature/Film Quarterly*. He has published several plays, more than four hundred poems, and two books of poetry: *Presently a Beast* (1996) and *Devilfish* (1999). Brewer recently won the Michael W. Gearhart Award in Poetry from *Sundog: The Southeast Review*.

Following Brewer's lead, John Bickley, a screenwriting intern at Fusion studios working toward a PhD in American Literature, has attempted to approach *Deconstructing Harry* with theoretical techniques. He finds the film fascinating and creative, and an attempt by the screenwriter to defend his own personal qualities and aesthetic decisions. Bickley, in revealing the postmodern concept of the fragmented self in his protagonist/novelist, displays an awareness of the mechanics of presentation which also undergird more recent films.

The final essay of the three concentrating on *Deconstructing Harry* has been written by the distinguished Sam Girgus, professor of English at Vanderbilt University and author of many books and articles. In 1992 he wrote a full-length study of Allen entitled *The Films of Woody Allen,* and three years earlier he published the important *Desire and the Political Unconscious in American Literature: Error and Ideology,* and prior to this volume, *The New Covenant: Jewish Writers and the American Idea* (1984). He has not written publicly on Allen's films in the past few years but his interpretation of *Deconstructing Harry* offers fresh insights into the artist's present interests. Among these interests appear to be a probing into entertainment conventions. In "Deconstructing *Everyone Says I Love You* and *Sweet and Lowdown*" I comment on certain cinematic and television genres that Allen satirizes and dissects in a loving way. Hence this essay attempts to explain Allen's attraction to certain genres while maintaining a sophisticated yet affectionate distance from his subject matter and its significance in American culture.

Concluding this volume is Eric Lax's reminiscence of conversations he has had with Woody Allen over the years. The author of *On Being Funny: Woody Allen and Comedy* (1975) and a biography of Humphrey Bogart in 1997, Lax's major contribution to Allen scholarship is his authoritative biography of the author in 1991, entitled *Woody Allen: A Biography,* making him one of the best known critics and commentators on the playwright and flimmaker. Therefore, "Conversations with Woody" reveals the relaxed but affirming bond that exists between artist and biographer.

Chronology

1935   Allan Stewart Konigsberg is born on December 1 to Nettie Cherry and Martin Konigsberg, who live in Brooklyn, New York.

1941   Konigsberg's parents enroll him in Brooklyn P.S. 99 instead of Hunter College's prestigious magnet school, for which his I.Q. qualifies him. Also in this year, Konigsberg takes his first, unforgettable trip to Manhattan.

1944   Sister, Letty, is born.

1944-1951   Konigsberg is enchanted by the movies his parents take him to see and grows especially enamoured of comedian Bob Hope. He also develops interests in magic and jazz. He enters Midwood High School in 1949 and hates it, barely passing his classes.

1951   Kongisberg performs as a stage magician in the Catskills at Weinstein's Majestic Bungalow Colony, but decides soon afterward to pursue comedy rather than magic.

1952   Konigsberg takes the name Woody Allen, using a form of his first name and adopting Woody because of its comical sound. His first jokes are published, without his name, by columnist Nick Kenny in the *New York Daily Mirror*.

1953   Allen begins working as a writer for the Alber press agency. He also sees Mort Sahl perform at the Blue Angel in New York and decides to pursue live comedy. He graduates from Midwood High School and enters New York University but often skips his classes, even in film, to go to movies. He is expelled from NYU, with the option of returning on academic probation in the summer of 1954.

1954   Allen enrolls in a film class at the City College of New York but does not finish the semester.

1955   Allen is laid off from the Alber agency and considers a career as a playwright or film director.

1956   Allen moves to Los Angeles to work on *The Colgate Variety Show* and invites Harlene Rosen to join him as his wife. They are married on March 15 and return to New York when the show closes a few months later. He spends the summer performing at the Tamiment summer resort in Pennsylvania.

1957   Allen performs again with great success at the Tamiment.

1958   Allen spends his third and final summer at the Tamiment. He also writes the *Chevy Show* with Larry Gelbart, for which they win the Sylvania Award and receive an Emmy nomination for it. Allen says he plans to retire but continues to produce.

1958   Allen writes a parody of Ingmar Bergman's *Wild Strawberries* for Art Carney's *Hooray for Love*. Also in this year, he begins Freudian psychoanalysis.

1959   Allen writes for *The Garry Moore Show* but hopes to get out of television. Two of his sketches are included in *From A to Z*, a revue performed at the Plymouth Theater. The revue is a failure, but agents Jack Rollins and Charles Joffe decide to represent Allen for an initial period of six months. Allen performs for the first time as a live comic at the Blue Angel, and the audience's cool response leads him nearly to give up the idea of performing live.

1960   Allen performs again at the Blue Angel to a more receptive audience. He travels cross-country performing in various clubs with increasing success and often earns $5,000 per performance.

1961   Woody and Harlene Allen divorce.

1962   Allen's popularity is noted in a *Newsweek* magazine article on up-and-coming comedians.

1963   The *New York Times* gives Allen's work a favorable review.

1964   Allen substitutes for Johnny Carson on the *Tonight Show* and earns up to $10,000 per week. He drafts *Lot's Wife*, an unsuccessful attempt at collaboration with Clive Donner.

1965   Allen's first film, *What's New, Pussycat?*, is received negatively by critics but ranks among the top five money-making films of the year.

1966   Allen marries Louise Lasser on February 2. He writes *Casino Royale* with Val Guest in London. Allen's play *Don't Drink the Water* and his film *What's Up, Tiger Lily?* open around the same time. The *New Yorker* magazine publishes his comic pieces "The Gossage-Varbedian papers" and "A Little Louder, Please."

1967   Allen and Mickey Rose begin working on a film adaptation of Richard Powell's novel *Don Quixote USA,* but abandon it to write *Take the Money and Run,* a parody of numerous recent documentaries about murderers.

1968   *Casino Royale* is released and becomes one of the top three money-makers of the year. Allen directs and stars in *Take the Money and Run* and begins casting the Broadway-bound *Play It Again, Sam.*

1969   Charles Joffe begins negotiating a contract with United Artists, which when later signed, provides both support and freedom for Allen's work. Allen's first United Artists picture, *Take the Money and Run,* is released to mixed reviews. *Don't Drink the Water,* a project Allen has not closely supervised, is released without great success. Allen uses part of his work for *Don Quixote USA* in a new script called *Bananas.* Allen and Lasser divorce in Mexico and Diane Keaton moves into Allen's New York apartment, though Allen continues to work with Lasser and does not end their relationship. Allen writes another Kraft special and invites the Rev. Billy Graham as his guest. Allen and Keaton appear on *The Tonight Show.*

1970   Allen and Diane Keaton separate but continue their relationship intermittently.

1971   *Bananas* opens to moderately favorable reviews.

1972   Allen shoots a film version of *Play it Again, Sam.* Allen makes the political satire *The Politics and Humor of Woody Allen* but it is deemed too controversial and is never broadcast. Allen writes *Everything You Always Wanted to Know About Sex* and tours in his own one-act show called *Death,* which he plans as the first of *Death, God, and Sex.*

1973   Allen experiments with science fiction in *Sleeper.*

1974   Allen writes *Love and Death,* filming it in Budapest and Paris, and
            works on *The Front,* a project in which he takes little pleasure.

1975   *Love and Death* is released.

1976   Allen films *Annie Hall,* under the working title *Anhedonia,* with
            great difficulty. He also acts in *The Front,* directed by Martin Ritt.

1977   *Annie Hall* is released with great popular success in spite of critical
            misgivings.

1978   *Annie Hall* garners Academy Awards for Best Film, Best Screen-
            play (Allen and Marshall Brickman), Best Actress (Diane Keaton),
            and Best Director (Allen). Allen does not attend the ceremony,
            playing jazz in New York instead.

1979   Allen directs *Interiors* in the style of Ingmar Bergman, but
            Bergman's *Autumn Sonata* eclipses Allen's project in the eyes of
            New York critics and, eventually, the Academy. Another collabora-
            tion with Brickman, *Manhattan,* opens to mostly very favorable re-
            views. Allen makes *Stardust Memories* about the difficulties of
            show business.

1980   *Stardust Memories* opens. Allen begins a relationship with Mia Far-
            row, who has several children (biological and adopted) from her
            previous marriage to conductor André Previn. Allen begins writing
            Zelig, his first effort for Orion.

1981   Allen writes *A Midsummer Night's Sex Comedy.*

1982   *A Midsummer Night's Sex Comedy* does not earn a significant re-
            turn, and its backers grow ambivalent about supporting Allen's
            work.

1983   Allen completes work on *Zelig,* which is well received in New York
            but fails elsewhere. He also begins shooting *Broadway Danny
            Rose.*

1984   *Broadway Danny Rose* fails to turn a profit in the United States but
            meets with more success in Europe.

1985   Allen's film *The Purple Rose of Cairo* is released, and reviewers re-
            spond positively to its American aesthetic. Allen also begins shoot-
            ing the complex *Radio Days.*

1986   *Hannah and Her Sisters* opens. The three sisters are based in part on Mia, Tisa, and Steffi Farrow. Allen responds to pressure from Orion to make the movie funnier. It receives enthusiastic reviews and enjoys great popular success.

1987   *Radio Days* and *September* open. *September* is Allen's least successful film. Allen begins filming *Another Woman.* Farrow gives birth to Allen's first child, Satchel, but the couple's relationship begins to deteriorate.

1988   *Another Woman* receives negative reviews. Allen films *Oedipus Wrecks,* a short film that eventually meets with little success, and begins filming *Brothers.*

1989   *Crimes and Misdemeanors* opens to receptive audiences and favorable reviews. Allen begins shooting *Alice* in spite of deep depression.

1990   Allen films *Scenes from a Mall* and begins expanding his one-act play *Death* into *Shadows and Fog.*

1991   *Scenes From a Mall* opens. Around this time, Allen begins a relationship with Soon-Yi Previn, Farrow's adopted daughter, and writes *Husbands and Wives,* a cynical satire of exploitative relationships. Allen adopts Moses, Farrow's only child without a biological or adoptive father on record, and her daughter, Dylan.

1992   *Shadows and Fog* opens to quiet reviews. *Husbands and Wives* opens on 865 screens. Allen and Farrow separate.

1993   *Husbands and Wives* performs well initially but then falters. Still, it wins Academy Awards nominations for Allen's screenplay and Judy Davis's Best Supporting Actress performance. *Manhattan Murder Mystery* earns a profit, reversing the decline in Allen's popularity since *Hannah and Her Sisters.* Allen begins writing *Bullets Over Broadway* with Doug McGrath.

1994   Allen's request for custody of Moses, Satchel (renamed Harmon, then Seamus), and Dylan (renamed Eliza) is denied. *Bullets Over Broadway* is released with great success.

1995   *Bullets Over Broadway* wins nominations for Best Original Screenplay and Best Director, best Art Director, Supporting Actor, Supporting Actress, and Actress (Dianne Wiest). Allen writes *Central*

Park West, a sketch within *Death Defying Acts,* which opens to mixed critical reviews. Allen's *The Sunshine Boys,* intended for American television, opens in Europe. Allen attempts his first musical, *Everyone Says I Love You.*

1996   *Mighty Aphrodite* proves unpopular in America in spite of Mira Sorvino's Academy Award for Best Supporting Actress. Allen takes a short tour with his New Orleans Jazz Band, filmed and released as *Wild Man Blues.*

1997   Allen wins the Leone d'Or at the Venice Film Festival for his work. He also films *Deconstructing Harry. The Sunshine Boys* is broadcast on American television.

1998   Allen and Soon-Yi Previn marry. He films *Celebrity.* He also appears in *The Imposters* and plays a voice role in *Antz.*

1999   *Sweet and Lowdown* opens.

Sources

Baxter, John. *Woody Allen.* London: HarperCollins, 1998.
Lax, Eric. *Woody Allen: A Biography.* New York: Knopf, 1991.
Torp, Anders Herman. *Woody Allen* Web Site. Available at HYPERLINK "http://www.idi.ntnu.no/~torp/woody/" *http://www.idi.ntnu.no/~torp/woody/* . Retrieved from the World Wide Web on February 15, 2000.

Song as Subtext
The Virtual Reality of Lyrics in the Films of Woody Allen

CAROL GOODSON

Although frequently mentioned in passing, few critics and reviewers have commented in detail on the prominent place which music holds in Woody Allen's films. Since Allen is a serious amateur jazz clarinetist, who even skipped the Oscar ceremonies the night *Annie Hall* won four awards, because the event was held on the evening he regularly plays with the band at Michael's Pub in New York City (McCann 134, 143), it seems a bit surprising that more attention has not been given to this aspect of his work.

In fact, music is so potent a force in Allen's life that he structured an entire film around songs, the lyrical *Radio Days* (1987). In a series of interviews conducted during 1992 and 1993 by Swedish filmmaker and journalist Stig Bjorkman, Allen explained that "I wanted to make a memory for each important song from my childhood. It was the way it happened. And when I started to write the memories of the songs, I got inspiration for other scenes and sequences which could strengthen and support these memories" (Allen 164). All told, *Radio Days* uses an amazing forty-one songs, each the theme for a vignette, only sometimes invented, from Allen's urban childhood during the late 1930s and early '40s—proving that at least in this case, songs essentially served as source texts for the film.

For many of the tunes used in *Radio Days*, we actually hear the lyrics being sung, and they serve as effective commentary for the events being depicted on the screen. When Little Joe enters the fabulous Radio City Music Hall for the first time in his life, on the soundtrack is a recording of Frank Sinatra singing "If You Are But a Dream." The words we hear,

> If you're a fantasy
> then I'm content to be
> in love with loving you
>
> . . . .
> I'm so afraid
> that you may vanish in the air,

capture perfectly the feelings that we imagine the onscreen Joe is experiencing; they give us a substantial clue to an interior state which cannot be expressed as fully through visualization alone. In *The Purple Rose of Cairo* (1985), Allen again uses song lyrics to emphasize a character's inner emotions, as we observe the lonely Cecilia watching Fred Astaire dance on the screen to the strains of "Cheek to Cheek." The words, "Heaven, I'm in heaven / And the cares that hung around me through the week / Seem to vanish like a gambler's lucky streak," accurately describe her situation, as she uses the movies to forget temporarily her bleak existence.

Even more interesting, however, are the songs for which we do <u>not</u> hear the lyrics, but which are so familiar that we know at least some of the words. For instance, at the beginning of *Radio Days*, we hear, more than see, two fumbling burglars with flashlights breaking into a totally dark house. Somewhere near them in the darkness, the phone rings; the thieves, in a panic, afraid the sound will wake up the neighbors, decide to answer. It turns out to be the host of a radio quiz show "Guess That Tune," asking them to identify a song to be played by the studio orchestra, in order to win a prize. The song we then hear is "Dancing in the Dark," and if the viewer does not know that, s/he will not get the joke quite so quickly.

After this humorous opening, the *Radio Days* "story" finally begins with a romantic, foggy, rainswept view of the ocean at Rockaway, and on the soundtrack we hear the music of "September Song." Again, while we are only hearing the beautiful music, our *minds* can't help but supply the familiar words:

> Oh it's a long, long while,
> from May to December;
> and the days grow short

when you reach September.
When the autumn weather
turns the leaves to flame,
one hasn't got time
for the waiting game.

Oh, the days dwindle down
to a precious few:
September . . . November . . . .

And these few precious days,
I'll spend with you;
these precious days,
I'll spend with you. (Weill 16–17)

Even if you don't know all of the words, you know enough to get it: *heard* in a subliminal sense, these lyrics serve as an effective subtext for the scene; they inform us that we are about to hear the reminiscences of a person at least middle-aged, nostalgic about the past, who realizes that life is inexorably drawing to a close. In the time left, this person wants to be sure to keep treasured memories alive, and to remain mentally and emotionally in the company of the long-dead people from childhood, who are, in many ways, more real and important than people of the present. Furthermore, the song lyrics allow Allen to convey ideas which would seem too sentimental and embarrassing if actually verbalized. His subtle technique adds a layer of virtual, unspoken text to the films. We can say that this text is *virtually real* because it doesn't exist in the film, only in the minds of the audience. Among other things, by putting these words into the minds of viewers without really having to say them out loud, he is able to express a warmer, more romantic side of his nature, without really "owning" it.

In the 1979 film *Manhattan*, it is impossible not to notice the music, which is entirely based on the works of George Gershwin. Annette Wernblad, one of those who does often comment on Allen's use of music, observes that "Allen's mythologizing of his city is emphasized by the Gershwin songs, the lyrics of which are used very precisely to correspond to the plot" (78). In another analysis of the film, Graham McCann mentions Allen's "readiness to surprise us with daring narrative techniques" (205), but does not seem to be counting his use of song subtexts among them, although he does remark that "Allen's choice of songs provides specific settings in which to interpret each scene" (205) and includes some examples. If one examines the film closely, however, it seems quite reasonable to assert that the songs are actually a substantial part of the complete text of the film and are yet another instance of Allen's continual search for innovative narrative strategies.

Perhaps this aspect of his artistry is largely ignored because so many critics dismiss him as a mere imitator of the great European masters of filmmaking, especially Bergman. While discussing Bergman, whom he admittedly does admire, Allen relates that "Bergman once said in an interview at some point that he felt the use of music in films was barbaric. That was the word he used. But I don't. I feel the use of music in films is a very, very important part of the tools that you're working with. Just like light and sound" (197). This hardly gives the impression of a director who hesitates to deviate from the model set by his predecessors, and it provides further evidence that Allen is indeed trying to use music in the way in which I am suggesting. An additional hint is supplied in *Annie Hall* (1977), when Alvy, talking to Annie about photography, says that "the medium enters in as a condition of the art form itself." Obviously, it is the same with filmmaking; a soundtrack is available, which can be used in a number of ways, as the director chooses; the fact that many filmmakers use music only behind the text as filler or mood-inducer does not obviate the fact that it *could* be used—and indeed, Allen *does* appear to use it—as an extension of the text itself. As a genre, film allows for and even invites the use of music as a subtext, and, moreover, we might well define a truly great work of art as one in which every facet contributes to its total effect.

Ever more subtle uses of lyrics as narrative subtext emerge in Allen's succeeding films. For example, in *Hannah and Her Sisters* (1986), the father plays the song "Bewitched, Bothered, and Bewildered" on the piano during the pre-Thanksgiving dinner socializing. The three categories mentioned in the title of the song (which is used repeatedly throughout the film and serves as underlying theme music) characterize the sisters' lives perfectly. Hannah is "bewitched" in that she seems to have been born under a lucky star: like an enchanted princess, everything goes right for her; "bothered" is Lee, the middle sister, who is being pursued by Elliott, Hannah's husband; and Holly, the youngest, is "bewildered," the one who just cannot seem to get her life together: after beating drug addiction, she is unable to find meaningful work to support herself and keeps borrowing money from Hannah in order to finance her latest vocational whim.

September (1987) opens with the music of the song, "Slow Boat to China"; all the characters staying at Lane's country house are trying to pretend that they are on a slow boat to China, isolated from their real lives and responsibilities. Lane is recovering from a nervous breakdown, Stephanie is trying to decide if she wants to stay married, and Peter has given himself one summer in which to try to fulfill his lifelong dream of writing a novel. Stephanie and Peter are very attracted to each other. After Peter declares his love, Stephanie retreats to the piano, and we hear a medley of songs which describe her mental state; first, "What'll I Do," as she wonders whether she should leave her husband and go away with Peter, then "Slow Boat to China" again, as she fantasizes about running away to Paris with him and ignoring her family obligations. Again, the point is, that the information we unconsciously absorb by involuntarily ingesting at least scraps of the song lyrics within our own heads, helps us to fully interpret the scene and identify more closely with the emotions of the characters. It is not necessary to cite example after example of the use of unsung song lyrics as additional text within Allen's cinematic work, for this is a notable feature of nearly all of his films, to one degree or another. The inevitable question which arises, though, is how and why did he develop this technique, and what else—besides elucidating the films—is behind this rather striking approach?

First, one must take into account Allen's personal history. He is a city dweller, for one thing; he remarked to Bjorkman that conversation is "what city life is. It's verbal communication. City life is cerebral" (Allen 79). For another, he began working as a writer first, then a stand-up co-median. In both of these occupations, verbal ability is paramount, and in-deed whenever Allen talks about his own early life, he always stresses the fact that he was (and still is) primarily a writer:

> I could always write. Even as a little child, I could make up good stories before I could even read. . . . Then I was hired to write when I was sixteen, when I was still in school. . . . And then I wrote for radio and television and cabaret comedians. And then I wrote for myself as a cabaret comedian. And then I wrote that film script and ultimately I directed. (8)

As he implies, Allen more or less "fell" into the film world when, based on his stand-up comedy performances, he was offered the chance to write the script for *What's New, Pussycat?* (1965)—and based on that limited amount of experience, the chance to work a year later on *What's Up, Tiger Lily?* (10, 15).

Wernblad notes that although *Tiger Lily* is certainly nothing for which Allen will be remembered, "in its plot structure and breaking of cinematic conventions, it anticipates some of Woody Allen's very best works. The idea of adding an asynchronous humorous soundtrack is developed in several of the later movies, as is the split screen technique" (26–27). Thus we see him very early in his career experimenting with soundtrack, using it to alter the meaning of a film, and radically changing the viewer's perception of what is seen on the screen. Soundtrack, for Allen, is already much more than mere background.

Allen openly admits that he learned how to make films on the job, and despite his lack of experience, it never occurred to him that he would not know what to do (Allen 19). However, he did have help along the way; for example, he began using records behind his films at the suggestion of editor Ralph Rosenblum, who told him that having some music accompanying the footage, even if it was not the final music for the film, would bring the film alive and make editing decisions easier. Eventually Allen noticed that he liked the effect of the records which he had been arbitrarily (and temporarily) sticking into his movies to help the editing process along:

> I like the sound of the records. I can control it, I can do the music myself, right here in this room. There are all my records over there. I just pick up the world's great music and melodies, and I can choose whatever I want . . .so I started doing that, and I never stopped. (34)

When asked if he plans the music before shooting the film, Allen replied that he usually does have songs in mind that he thinks will be right for it, and that he has sometimes "filmed scenes that in themselves might not mean anything, but I knew that later, when I put the music behind it, the combination would be good" (35), which clearly indicates that he expects the lyrics to help make the meaning of the scene apparent to the audience. Allen has been quoted as saying that "contemporary conflicts are within yourself. . . . They're much less clearly visual." (61).

When we put all these facts together, it seems reasonable to suppose that making the transition to a visual medium from a verbal one may have been somewhat difficult for Allen. On this basis, one might also hypothesize that his use of song lyrics is at least partly based on the deeply felt need of an artist who is a writer by instinct, to add a level of text to film which normally is not there. Indeed, at least one critic has commented that "the problem is that Allen's comedy is still designed for reading or hearing, rather than watching" (McCann 69). An intriguing sidelight is contained in his remarks to Bjorkman on the subject of subtitles in foreign films:

> I've had a funny problem over the years in that the films I like so much are foreign films. And they have subtitles. So you read them. When I write my dialogue for certain films, I'm almost writing it in a way you would a subtitle, rather than human-speak. It's an odd little problem. (117)

In *The Act of Reading*, literary theorist Wolfgang Iser offers some additional insight into Allen's probable intentions, when he notes that the interaction of reader and author involves a sharing in

> the game of the imagination, and, indeed, the game will not work if the text sets out to be anything more than a set of governing rules. The reader's enjoyment begins when he himself becomes productive, i.e., when the text allows him to bring his own faculties into play. (108)

Quoting Sartre, who refers to the relationship between reader and author as a "pact," Iser tells us that the process of writing includes the dialectic of reader/writer, which absolutely *requires* the presence of two people in order to bring the work of art into existence (108). Allen's use of song lyrics in the way I have described involves the reader in an effort of co-authorship, as s/he mentally supplies the words to songs for which only the melodies are heard, and then in imagination adds those unspoken texts to the formal, expressed text presented on the screen, thus creating a complete work of art.

Perhaps the most important reason that Allen utilizes song as subtext has not yet been considered, and that is his desire to perpetuate an important aspect of American culture which he sees as in danger of being lost. In *Hannah and Her Sisters*, there is a humorous but telling episode in which Mickey and Holly have a disastrous date. She insists on going to a club to hear some New Wave music, which he finds incomprehensible and far below the level of what he would consider to be musical art. In response he then takes *her* to the Cafe Carlyle to experience the exquisite cabaret/jazz piano of Bobby Short, and now the shoe is on the other foot—she hates it! Just as music's vital importance to Allen personally, is a given —especially the music of the 1920s through 1940s —there are also many indications in his interviews, of the low opinion he has of contemporary American culture (including its music) in comparison to what it was in the past. In Robert Benayoun's *The Films of Woody Allen*, he commented:

> I think popular culture in America has become another kind of junk food; our television, our music, most of our films, our politicians, our architecture, most of it is very mediocre and junky. And it is too bad, because we have the money, the technical knowledge. We could have had the greatest culture, but people are drugged by television, by cocaine, by whatever. (162)

In this context, no one should be surprised to learn that Allen told Bjorkman that one of Allen's two favorite poets is T. S. Eliot (200) and that the other was W. B. Yeats. Like Eliot, Allen strives to preserve a culture he sees as valuable and threatened. In the music for *Radio Days* there is an implicit suggestion that American culture is every bit as good, and on the same level as European. Annette Wernblad notes that over the credits, we hear Rimsky-Korsakov's "Flight of the Bumble Bee" played by Harry James; in this way, Allen "cleverly uses a piece of music which inherently juxtaposes nineteenth-century European highbrow culture with a twentieth-century American popular culture" (118). Furthermore McCann has noted that Allen, like Eliot, uses his musical allusions to this culture as a way of challenging his audience, an audience which is known to be discriminating, middle-class, educated, and primarily urban (197) —and one which includes the most important person of all, himself: "I make films for my own enjoyment" (81). Allen is like Eliot in another way too, if one considers that he seems to employ songs deliberately in the mode of the "objective correlative," using them to elicit specific emotions in his viewers.

The lyricists whom Allen invites into his films as co-authors are like omniscient narrators, in that they apparently know what's going on in the story, even when the characters may not. The use of song as subtext also allows him to bring alternate or supplementary texts directly into interaction with his own text, enabling him to go much deeper into levels of meaning than the mere evocation of parallels or sources can do. Similarly, Nancy Pogel has applied Mikhail Baktin's analysis of the dialogic novel (in which one text intersects with another, providing commentary on it) to Allen's films, maintaining that he uses this technique frequently and effectively (8).

One possible conclusion which can be drawn from all this is that ultimately, both the dialogic, self-referential technique and the use of unheard lyrics as subtext are part of Woody Allen's psychological self-defense—sophisticated narrative strategies which allow him to conceal himself from those who might ridicule him as a sentimental hack if he were to openly display the romantic person one can glimpse under the surface of his films, a person very much out of sync with the harsh and cynical world of today. If one listens to his films with the inner ear, attuned to the virtual reality present within, it is likely that the viewer may discover that the real Woody Allen is someone quite different from the public persona he has so carefully cultivated over the years.

Works Cited

Allen, Woody. *Woody Allen on Woody Allen*. Edited by Stig Bjorkman. 1993. New York: Grove, 1995.

Benayoun, Robert. *The Films of Woody Allen*. New York: Harmony Books, 1986.

Iser, Wolfgang. *The Act of Reading: A Theory of Aesthetic Response*. 1976. Baltimore: Johns Hopkins University Press, 1980.

McCann, Graham. *Woody Allen: New Yorker*. 1990. Cambridge, UK: Polity, 1991.

Pogel, Nancy. *Woody Allen*. Boston: Twayne, 1987.

Weill, Kurt. "September Song." (c1938) *Sheet Music Magazine* 5 (Apr./May 1981): 14–17.

Wernblad, Annette. *Brooklyn Is Not Expanding: Woody Allen's Comic Universe*. Rutherford, NJ: Fairleigh Dickinson University Press, 1992.

Self-Reflexivity in Woody Allen's Films

SAGE HAMILTON ROUNTREE

With the development of generic conventions, narrative forms quickly become self-conscious because writers working within a particular form must be aware of the genre's constitutive elements. Writing in each genre reflects this self-awareness. For example, Laurence Sterne's *Tristram Shandy* focuses on Shandy's writing; Thomas Kyd's *Spanish Tragedy* reaches its climax in a play-within-a-play based on the conventions of the revenge tragedy. Feature films have followed the same metanarrative path in the twentieth century—films such as *Footlight Parade* (1933) or 1941's *Sullivan's Travels* focus on moviemaking. But in recent years, that focus has become more pointed. With postmodernist self-reflexiveness, many films base their existence on examining the means by which they are constructed. In reflecting on their own construction, these films raise questions about artifice and reality and stress the relationship between the director and the viewer while following the same pattern of self-awareness other genres historically have exhibited. For example, Federico Fellini's *8 1/2* (1963) and Woody Allen's *Stardust Memories* (1980) both pay attention to directors' creative struggles; *The Player* (Robert Altman, 1992) and *The Muppet Movie* (Jim Henson, 1979), are so self-aware their narratives circle back upon themselves seamlessly.

An examination of metanarrative and self-reflexive techniques in film, and films' use of different narrative elements and temporality, can lead us toward a greater understanding of the metanarrative potentials of the cinema. Woody Allen's work contains many of these metanarrative elements. His films refer to the magic of movies and to the process of filmmaking (*The Purple Rose of Cairo*), to an author's or director's

11

struggles with the parallels between art and life (*Deconstructing Harry*), and, in the case of *Stardust Memories* (1980) and *Crimes and Misde-meanors* (1989), to themselves in a self-begetting fashion. A considera-tion of metanarrative techniques in these and other films will lead us to a greater appreciation of film's potential for reconsidering and revising tra-ditional conventions both of cinema and of narrative as a whole.

When the cinema emerged as one of the newest media for conveying narrative, it began to establish its own boundaries as a narrative form. Unlike the theater, where the audience creates a fourth wall that limits narrative possibilities, and where a sense of scene and temporal continu-ity relies heavily on the imagination of the audience, the cinema ex-panded the narrative abilities of drama in a new dimension. Along with the new narrative techniques, a metanarrative of the cinema developed. The metanarrative impulse in films occurs both as this historically typi-cal progression coming early in the development of the art form, and as a reflection of a generally postmodern trend toward self-reflexiveness. But while readers, especially of postmodern novels, are constantly aware of the process of reading, the viewer who prepares to watch a film usually prepares to suspend disbelief and concentrate on the story of the movie, not the way in which it was produced. Metanarrative films, however, force an audience's attention toward their status as constructions by de-picting the various elements that go into making a film and examining the way in which narrative is created.

Metafictions are more concerned with narrative itself than with imi-tation of life. Through the course of creating a fictional narrative, they deconstruct that narrative and examine its components. Many metanarra-tive films use frames to set up their stories. Patricia Waugh argues that the effect of frame breaks, "instead of *reinforcing* our sense of a continu-ous reality, is to split it open, to *expose* the levels of illusion. We are forced to recall that our 'real' world can *never* be the 'real' world of the novel. So the frame-break, while appearing to bridge the gap between fiction and reality, in fact lays it bare" (33). This metafictive effect is also achieved in metanarrative films, where various filmic or diegetic levels act as frames.

According to Gerald Prince, "A narrative having [a] narrative as [one of] its topics is [a] metanarrative. More specifically, a narrative re-ferring to itself and to those elements by which it is constituted and com-municated, a self-reflexive narrative, is metanarrative" (51). This definition provides a subcategory to the metanarrative, the self-reflexive. A self-reflexive narrative is self-aware, self-consciously acknowledging the mechanisms that make it a narrative. Waugh writes that "Metafictional novels tend to be constructed on the principle of a fundamental and sustained opposition: the construction of a fictional illusion (as in traditional realism) and the laying bare of that illusion. In other words, the lowest common denominator of metafiction is simultaneously to create a fiction and to make a statement about the creation of that fiction" (6). The lowest common denominator of metafiction, then, is self-reflexivity. This can be accomplished by many techniques—often, for example, a glance directly into the camera constitutes a self-reflexive moment. Characters describing the movie they are in, as Judah Rosenthal does in *Crimes and Misdemeanors*, lend self-reflexivity to a film.

Crimes and Misdemeanors does not purport to be about filmmaking, although one of its characters, Clifford Stern (Allen) is a filmmaker and film buff; it does not purport to be about moviegoing, although Clifford takes both his niece and his love interest, Hally Reed (Mia Farrow) to the movies as a bonding device. The film does use quick jumps to clips of movies to underscore the action, but always pulls back to show Clifford at the theater. For example, when Judah Rosenthal (Martin Landau) considers taking a hit out on his renegade mistress, Dolores (Angelica Huston), a scene from *This Gun's for Hire* appears on the screen; when the detective pays Judah a visit after Dolores's murder, Allen cuts to a song from *Happy Go Lucky*: "He says murder, he says."

The two story lines of the film, those of Judah's dilemma and Clifford's infatuation with Hally, seem only tangentially related, but they come together in the final scene. Late at Rabbi Ben's daughter's wedding, Judah and Clifford meet in a back room, as Clifford is seething over Hally's engagement to his soon-to-be-ex-brother-in-law, Lester. "I was planning the perfect murder," he tells Judah, who asks, "Movie plot?" Judah then recapitulates his story for Clifford:

> Let's say there's this man who is very successful. He has everything . . . and after the awful deed is done he finds that he's plagued by deep-rooted guilt. Little sparks of his religious background, which he'd rejected, are suddenly stirred up . . . now he's panic stricken, on the verge of a mental collapse, an inch away from confessing the whole thing to the police; and then one morning he awakens and the sun is shining and his family is around him, and mysteriously the crisis is lifted. He takes his family on a vacation to Europe and as the months pass he finds he's not punished. In fact, he prospers. The killing gets

attributed to some person, a drifter who has a number of other murders to his credit . . . now he's scot-free. His life is completely back to normal, back to his protected world of wealth and privilege.

This conversation in the denouement of Jonah's story, filling in the resolution brought by the four months that pass before the film's final scene. But it also provides a commentary on the story's narrative arc. When Clifford posits that the man in the story would have problems living with his deed, Jonah argues, "This is reality. In reality we rationalize, we deny, or we couldn't go on living." Clifford proposes a different ending: "I'd have him turn himself in, because then your story assumes tragic proportions, because in the absence of a god, he is forced to assume that responsibility himself. Then you have tragedy." In the film's most self-reflexive statement, Jonah reminds Clifford, "But that's fiction. That's movies. You've seen too many movies. If you want a happy ending, you should go see a Hollywood movie," and he laughs. Thus this film—not a Hollywood movie per se, but certainly a piece of art and not "reality"—presents itself as a mirror to nature, as an example of "real life," while at the same time self-reflexively acknowledging its status as a construction.

What happens to narrative when an entire film is self-reflexive; that is, when the whole film deals with the mechanisms, conventions, and motivations by which it itself is created? The result it not just a film-within-a-film, although that is a common by-product of metanarrative effects; the resulting movie will be a film about the very film it is. It will be *self-begetting*. In a self-begetting film, the story we watch on the screen is itself the reason we are watching it. The film deals with the motivation for its own production. A self-begetting film might have any number of diegetic, or filmic, levels, as it can contain flashbacks and flashes forward, as well as memory and fantasy sequences. It will always have, however, a first filmic level and a zero filmic level. These two levels correspond in some ways to the *story* and *discourse* studied in narratology.[1] The story is the bare elements of the narrative, the Burkean who, what, where, when. The discourse is the narrative realization of the story. The discourse is the narrative we read or see; it is the text. In a self-begetting film, the zero filmic level corresponds to the story. It is the reason for what we are watching, and it contains the particulars of the plot. The first filmic level is the discourse, the demonstration of the elements of the story, and the action we see on the screen for the majority of the film, excluding memory and fantasy sequences. The zero level is the underlying story, the story of how this film came to be made, which we see enacted at the first filmic level. The zero level is often introduced or alluded to in a frame, either at the start of the film or, more commonly, at the end—just as Allen does at the end of *Stardust Memories*.

Woody Allen's tenth picture, *Stardust Memories* contains an elaborate mix of narrative elements. Fantasy, present action, films-within-the-film, and, most importantly, memories all mix to create a metanarratively complicated film. It begins with a Fellini-esque fantasy. We see Allen's character, Sandy Bates, on a train filled with dirty, solemn, sad people. The train on the next track is full of happy, beautiful people. A beautiful woman (Sharon Stone, in one of her first roles) blows him a kiss, and the trains begin to move. Sandy desperately tries to explain to the conductor that he is on the wrong train, but he is too late. Next, we see the crowd from the dingy train wandering around a dump, with seagulls flying overhead. It is a depressing, pessimistic opening.

The next scene reveals that the previous has been a film. Since it is part of a completed film, it exists in the past. We see silhouettes behind a movie screen and hear their voices, "Well, I thought it was terrible. . . . He's not funny anymore. . . . I've seen it all before. They try to document their private suffering and fob it off as art." These are the voices of Sandy's cronies—his producer and production company members. They accompany him to his apartment, where he asks if his girlfriend Isobel has called and worries, "Who needs a festival of my old films?" Sandy is about to leave for the New Jersey shore, for a weekend festival of his films at the Hotel Stardust. In this scene, we are at the first filmic level. The action is taking place in the present. This has been pointed out by the switch from the early film-fantasy to the scene in Sandy's apartment. When his cronies leave, Sandy remembers his ex-girlfriend Dorrie. This switches the filmic level yet again, as a new narrative element—flash-back—is introduced with Sandy's memories.

Soon Sandy arrives at the Stardust, where his fans mob him, delighted to see him. One exclaims, "I especially like your early funny [films]!" There is a quick cut to an odd vision Sandy has of a boy with his mother. It is a purely atemporal image, unidentifiable as either fantasy or memory, yet it reveals something about Sandy. Perhaps he is imagining a new film. Inside the Stardust, Sandy calls Isobel and invites her to join him for the weekend. This again reminds us of Fellini's *8 1/2*, as Guido invited both his mistress and wife to the spa to join him.

At the first night's screening, the rabid fans ask questions of Sandy, who answers them with jokes ("What were you trying to say in this picture?" "I was just trying to be funny!"). While the fans ask questions,

Sandy remembers an image of Dorrie in the mental hospital. When he leaves the screening room, he speaks with his producer on the phone, "No, they can't recut my film!" The scene from the opening of *Stardust Memories*, it turns out, is a work-in-progress. While the fans press Sandy to donate his time and objects to charity, or attempt to have a word with him, he meets a screenwriting teacher, Jack, and his classical violinist girlfriend, Daisy. They all go for a beer. At the roadhouse, the Felliniesque entertainers evoke a flashback memory-fantasy in Sandy. He envisions "The amazing Sandy," a young boy who performs magic tricks for an adoring audience. On the first filmic level, in the present, Sandy is attracted to Daisy because she reminds him of Dorrie.

After returning to the hotel, Sandy remembers his first meeting with Dorrie, who, we learn here, was an actress working on one of his films. He sees her on the beach, sitting in a chair under a scaffolding evocative of *8 1/2*'s launching pad. They are shown recording various scenes of a film. Each shot involves a dramatic action—a kiss, a slap—and the camera pulls back to reveal that they are acting for a movie camera. These are positive memories of Dorrie, and the sequence culminates in a memory of a pigeon flying into Sandy's apartment, frightening him, making Dorrie laugh.

Back in the present, Sandy enters his hotel room to find a woman in his bed, ready to sleep with him. Flustered, he tells her to leave, and we hear a voice-over: "We interrupt this program with a special bulletin. Sydney Finkelstein's anger has escaped!" This is obviously a film Sandy has made previously, since we see him, but he's playing a character named Sydney Finkelstein. We hear the laughter of the Stardust audience at the huge gorilla-like creature, purportedly Finkelstein's anger, on the rampage through the forest. The film clip is followed by another question and answer session; Sandy is again besieged by adoring fans in the hotel lobby.

At this point, we believe we have a fairly good understanding of the various narrative elements at play here, since we have grown accustomed to recognizing the difference between memory, fantasy, and Sandy's film clips. *Stardust Memories* continues, however, to mix these elements up further. Isobel arrives at the hotel and announces that she has left her husband. Sandy is taken aback, and wonders about the future of their relationship. This episode with Isobel is followed by a meeting with Daisy in the empty theater, emphasizing the potential for romance between Sandy and Daisy. Since Daisy reminds Sandy of Dorrie, a memory follows of manic-depressive Dorrie at one of her depressive moments. Back at the first filmic level, Sandy and Isobel visit his sister. The women look at a photo album, which triggers more memories.

There is a sudden cut to an image of a jazz orchestra playing on a cloud. The passengers from the train at the start of the movie wander around them, bewildered. We hear Sandy's voice, outraged: "What is that? Those are all the people from the train!" The producers announce that we are looking at "Jazz Heaven," the new ending to Sandy's movie. He protests, "The whole point of the movie is that no one is saved!" He and Isobel leave the lunch meeting, indignant. He tells Isobel he wants her to move in with him, but she is hesitant. This conversation leads to a clip from another film. Sandy is talking about his fantasy of switching the brains of two women, making a perfect woman . . . and then falling in love with the other one. We hear the audience's laughter and understand that this is a film shown at the festival.

In the next scene, Sandy visits with a friend who reminds him of the difficulties of dealing with Dorrie. He returns to his room to find Isobel asleep. We cut to a quick scene where Sandy tells his producers that it's immoral to change the end of his film. Next, Isobel's children arrive. At the train station restaurant, Sandy looks out the window and lapses into a memory of Dorrie. Isobel and Sandy run into Jack and Daisy, and agree that Sandy and Daisy will go to a showing of *The Bicycle Thief* in town. Here is a different kind of metanarrative moment, as the characters sit in the theater and later discuss the film, one of the most important films in the history of the cinema. Coincidentally, in *The Player*, Griffin Hill meets the writer David Kahane at a showing of *The Bicycle Thief*. Both of these metanarrative movies pay passing tribute to the giant of the neorealist films, a school where presentation of reality is key—but a neorealist film would never acknowledge the devices by which it became a film.

After leaving the movie, Sandy and Daisy wander into an empty ballroom, where he is approached by a woman claiming to be his mother. We are surprised, and then learn that she has only played his mother in a film. The woman asks about Dorrie, and triggers another memory of Dorrie in a depressive stage. Daisy is interested, and in the car, asks him, "How do I remind you of Dorrie?" He explains that both have a "lost" feeling to them. The car breaks down, and they stumble across a group of characters throwing a "UFO party" in a field. They all accost Sandy, discussing his films.

Here we see a crisis of filmic elements. Sharon Stone, the girl who blew a kiss from the other train at the start of the film, blows Sandy another from the front seat of a pickup truck. One of the UFO watchers tells

Sandy, " . . . you know, this is exactly like one of your satires. It's like we're all characters in some film being watched in God's screening room." The man is then grabbed from behind by the monster we recognize as Sydney Finkelstein's anger, in a convergence of filmic levels. Sandy makes Daisy float horizontally, in an impromptu magic trick. His parents, sister, and secretary appear, as well as his friend, who asks, "Do you remember the last time you saw [Dorrie]?" There is quick cut to a series of images of Dorrie in a mental institution, looking directly into the camera, and therefore at Sandy, as she talks to him in their last visit together.

After this painful memory, Sandy visits with a number of aliens, in what is pure fantasy. He asks them, "Why am I bothering to make films or anything?" They answer, "We enjoy your films, particularly the early, funny ones," echoing the words of a fan upon Sandy's arrival at the Hotel Stardust. The aliens advise him to stay with Isobel, telling him her womanly maturity beats Dorrie's insecurity. Sandy tells the aliens, "I've got to find meaning," and they disappear. More confused than ever, Sandy returns to the group and kisses Daisy. Immediately, Isobel, Jack, the hotel hostess, and the police show up, and Sandy walks away with Isobel, telling her he doesn't want to get married. In the middle of his explanation, a fan walks up to them, says, "Sandy, you know you're my hero," pulls out a pistol, and shoots him at close range.

We see the ambulance racing to the hospital, where, in the emergency room, with an anxious Isobel standing over him, Sandy Bates is pronounced dead. "Poor fool," the nurse says, "He's dead and he never found out the meaning of life!" Cut to a screen filled with the image of molten lava. A psychiatrist talks about Sandy's life, observing, "As one great Hollywood producer said, 'Too much reality is not what the people want.'" The woman in charge of the film festival introduces a film in which Sandy Bates plays God. She presents him with a posthumous award, and he appears to receive the plaque. He begins, "Just a little while back, just before I died . . . ," and describes a memory of a moment with Dorrie. They were listening to Louie Armstrong play "Stardust," and, for that moment, "I felt happy . . . almost indestructible." This, then, is the influential "Stardust" memory that has been haunting Sandy. Sandy has been trying to return to that happiness he felt with Dorrie that day, but he must accept that Dorrie was much more trouble than fun, and that he must choose a new life with Isobel instead of dwelling in the past, living through his memories.

A cut back to the emergency room reveals that the last scenes have been a fantasy. Sandy awakens, calling for Dorrie, and upsets Isobel, who leaves. The doctor explains that Sandy has merely fainted and "had some fantasy of being shot." The police have found a pistol in his car, however, and he is briefly thrown in jail.

When he is released, he catches up with Isobel and her children at the train station. He follows them onto a train similar to the train at the start of the film. Sandy tries to convince Isobel not to leave him:

> I had a very, very remarkable idea for a new ending for my movie. . . . We're on a train and there are lots of sad people on it . . . and I have no idea where it's headed . . . could be a junkyard, but it's not as bad as I originally thought it was, because we like each other and we have some laughs and there's a lot of closeness, and the whole thing is a lot easier to—There's this character that's based on you, and you're very warm and very giving, and you're absolutely nuts over me . . . and you're in love with me, and despite the fact that I do a lot of foolish things, you realize that down deep I'm not evil, just sort of floundering around, just searching, maybe. OK? . . . I know one thing, that a huge, big, wet kiss would go a long way toward selling this idea. I'm very serious, I think this is a big, big finish.

They kiss, the train begins to roll, and we hear applause. Sandy's speech has revealed what we have seen thus far to be a discrete movie in and of itself, his latest work. Isobel has been a character based on a "real life" woman. This self-reflexive speech even acknowledges that it is a "big finish."

The lights come up in the Stardust's theater. We hear the audience criticizing the film they have just seen, which we realize now has been the entirety of what we have just watched. Fans similar to those on the first filmic level appear now at this pseudo-zero level (originally the hypothetical zero filmic level, it is now the first filmic level), with such astounding insights as "What did you think the significance of the Rolls Royce is?" "I think that represents his car." But in addition to these characters, we see the actors who played roles in the film we have just seen discussing it. The actresses who played Daisy and Isobel commiserate about Sandy's kissing style. The audience files out, and Sandy Bates/Woody Allen enters, picks up his sunglasses—a symbol of fame—puts them on, and walks out of the darkening theater.

Closure is reached through the revelation of the artifice of the film we have just seen. The reunion of Sandy and Isobel brings that story to a close, promising that they will have a future together, showing that

Sandy has chosen Isobel over his memories of Dorrie. While that choice concludes the first filmic level, closure is doubly reached when the audience of actors is revealed. We quickly realize that what we have seen is finished, a completed film made by these actors. The purpose of *Stardust Memories* is the last minute or so, where the audience sorts out the filmic elements, to achieve a strong sense of closure.

Allen denies that the character, Sandy, is based on himself. Audience reaction to the film was fairly negative, as people thought Sandy Bates's attitude toward his public corresponded to Allen's own. He protests, in his interview with Stig Björkman: "They thought that the lead character was *me*! Not a fictional character, but me, and that I was expressing hostility toward my audience. And, of course, that was in no way the point of the film . . . I've never been the character I've played" (121-2). Parallels can be drawn, however, between Allen's status as a director and his character Sandy's status, although not as strongly as the parallels between Guido and Fellini in *8 1/2*, Allen admits the film has Fellini-esque tones. When Björkman suggests the opening train sequence in Allen's film echoes the traffic jam which starts *8 1/2*, Allen contrasts them: "Mine was more philosophically metaphoric, whereas in *8 1/2* it was a personal character trait of the lead character in the movie" (123). Both scenes introduce us to the psychological traits and mindsets of the director-characters, though, and the characters' dissatisfaction with their situations leads to some of the metanarrative—suggesting that if a director is unhappy with his work, he will push the envelope and attempt a different type of narrative.

Where do narrative elements exist in *Stardust Memories*? On the first filmic level, we finally decide, there is the film we have been watching for most of the time—the one we were watching along with the actors who saw themselves on the screen at the Stardust. Then, we must conclude, the frame Allen leaves us with at the end is a kind of filmic level zero. It cannot be the true zero level, as that is hypothetical, but it represents the zero level. The actors commenting on Allen's technique at the end are on our level; we have just shared the experience of watching *Stardust Memories* with them, after all. The various films-within-the-film, the movies Allen was commenting upon for the fans at the Stardust during the retrospective weekend, constitute a second filmic element. At times we have been tricked into considering them first filmic level, but we later realized they belong in a different category. Memories are a third narrative element, and a fourth is made up of a few stark images which can't be classified as either memory or fantasy. Temporality is repeatedly switched as Sandy remembers his past with Dorrie. Story time in the film encompasses a series of years, from Sandy's affair with Dorrie to his relationship with Isobel. The frame revealed at the end has its own temporality implied, since it must have taken time to bring the *Stardust Memories* we have seen to the screen the actors are watching at the end.

Stardust Memories continuously re-creates itself, taking the form of each of the films at the retrospective, then finally deciding to undercut its own narrative existence through the last scene. When the camera shows us that what we have been seeing is in itself a movie, shown to another audience, it creates a movie, but that movie encompasses what we have seen. What we have seen is a movie that wraps up all the movies discussed during the course of the action, not one that is the embodiment of all the movies we've seen in the course of watching *Stardust Memories*. In *Stardust Memories* Allen is not exactly making a film about another film; rather, he's making a film about reviewing a number of other films he has made previously. While Fellini's *8 1/2* is a film about a film that never begins, *Stardust Memories* is about a number of films which are complete. Nevertheless, both *8 1/2* and *Stardust Memories* show the variety of filmic elements available to metanarrative cinema. These movies examine the way in which a director can work with the elements of filmic narrative to explore the medium of film itself. This leads to a complicated assortment of narrative elements and a jumbled sense of "reality," while still uniting all of the films-within-the-film in the final overarching narrative.

These metanarrative techniques, both in *Crimes and Misdemeanors* and *Stardust Memories* draw attention to the entire process of suspension of disbelief. Cinemagoers are accustomed to ignoring the processes that go into making a film. They not only suspend their disbelief, they feel a persistence of vision as the film flickers by, ignoring the technical aspects of filmmaking in favor of the narrative unity a film provides. Metanarrative films, however, consistently draw attention to the means by which they are created. This foregrounding of form forces the viewer to acknowledge that the film is nothing but a series of images accompanied by sound. The audience must consider not only the technical aspects of filmmaking but also the motivations that lead to the production of a film. The director of a metanarrative film can speak more directly to the audience because he or she commands their attention through increasing their awareness of narrative elements. Thus, metanarrative in the cinema is an important technique, demanding that the viewers consider the form of film and identify with the directors—metanarrative in film increases our awareness of the possibilities of the cinema as an art form.

Notes

1. These are the commonly used terms cited by Prince. Mieke Bal uses fabula and story, respectively, to describe these two levels of narrative (see On Story-Telling: Essays in Narratology. Sonoma, Calif.: Polebridge Press, 1991).

Works Cited

Björkman, Stig. *Woody Allen on Woody Allen*. New York: Grove Press, 1995.
Prince, Gerald. *A Dictionary of Narratology*. Lincoln: University of Nebraska Press, 1987.
Waugh, Patricia. *Metafiction: The Theory and Practice of Self-Conscious Fiction*. London: Methuen, 1984.

Woody Allen
The Relationship Between The Persona And Its Author

MARIE-PHOENIX RIVET

Although Woody Allen's movies belong to very different genres ranging from comedy to drama, they stage the same types of characters and the same themes or sources of inspiration. One of their major characteristics is the persistence of the character whose role Woody Allen performed himself most of the time, but had sometimes interpreted by other actors: his persona.

For a long time the persona was the central character in Woody Allen's films. Most characters, especially male characters, were set up in the light of, or in the shadow of, the persona. From *A Midsummer Night's Sex Comedy* (1982), but essentially from multiple-plot movies such as *Hannah and Her Sisters* (1986), the persona did not necessarily have a prominent role. Moreover, the persona is not entirely linked to Woody Allen, who had it frequently played by actors other than himself. For example, in *Bullets over Broadway* (1994), John Cusack performed it. Gena Rowlands represented it in *Another Woman* (1988), as Mia Farrow had done in several movies, among others *The Purple Rose of Cairo* (1985). In *Celebrity* (1998), it is movie director Kenneth Branagh who fills the role.

In a movie made by Princeton University in 1977, the year when *Annie Hall* was released—at a period when the director was maturing and the persona was evolving—Woody Allen talks about creativity and about the origin of his persona. He asserts that his persona's creation was not intentional:

> I never set out to create any kind of image at all when I started
> as a comedian. I just did those jokes that I thought were funny. .
> . . It's never a choice you make, a conscious choice. . . . Some-
> thing occurs to you, seemingly at random. . . . I wanted to be a
> playwright when I started. I wrote for television, thinking I
> would write for television for some years and then gradually
> evolve into a playwright. (*Woody Allen: An American Comedy*)

It is striking that Allen considers events to occur "by themselves", as if
he did not have any influence on their course. In the same Princeton film,
Woody Allen refers to the difficulty of not getting influenced, of not becoming a "chameleon-man." Yet, so many traces of the influences ex-
erted on the filmmaker can be found in the persona: his admiration for
cinema's early silent comedians, his Jewish social and cultural background, but also his own personal and professional experience.

We could think that the persona was devised from Woody Allen's
rather unprepossessing physique, and that Woody Allen later on developed his verbal skills. Surprisingly, Woody Allen's humor was originally
purely verbal. As a child, he already wrote short stories which he used to
tell his classmates. At the age of fifteen, his skills as a humorist were acknowledged and paid for when he began to write one-liners for newspa-
pers. In 1961, he became a stand-up comedian, performing in Greenwich
Village nightclubs, though he was not a success from the start. He became aware that his writing was not enough to make people laugh; that
he needed to develop qualities other than verbal to be accepted as a comedian and be appreciated by the audience. The persona was not born
naturally, instinctively, but rather was constructed.

> However, Allen's creation of the persona was certainly molded
> by his physique: unattractive according to classic aesthetic val-
> ues, he is short, looks weak and is short-sighted, which compels
> him to wear glasses constantly. However, Woody Allen accentu-
> ated his seeming disadvantages to construct his persona: not
> only did he not hide his short-sightedness by wearing contact
> lenses but he even took advantage of it, wearing the same huge
> horn-rimmed glasses which became part of his "identity"
> rapidly. This is expressly in the image of what Harold Lloyd
> had done earlier.

Although some cinema theorists like Gerald Mast think that Woody
Allen's style is closer to the style of French filmmakers such as Jacques

Tati (Mast 313), his persona's type of humor places Woody Allen in the tradition of American silent movie comedians such as Harold Lloyd, Charles Chaplin, Buster Keaton, or Harry Langdon. Allen uses the techniques of silent cinema to build his earlier movies which revolve around his character and keep certain aspects of the silent clowns' personae to devise his own persona's features. Like his predecessors, he developed a persona which goes beyond the scope of a single movie. Allen himself admits that his persona was molded after a standard type set up by earlier movie comedians. In Stig Björkman's *Woody Allen on Woody Allen*, he confesses:

> Well, it seemed to me like a very standard film persona for a comedian. Someone who is a physical coward, who lusts after women, who is good-hearted but ineffectual and clumsy and nervous. All standard things that you've seen in different various disguises. In Charlie Chaplin or in W. C. Fields or Groucho Marx, there's the same thing, but in different forms. But the structural underbase was the same thing, as I view it. (26)

Some gags have been directly inspired by W. C. Fields, such as the gag in *Take the Money and Run* when Virgil Starkwell, the character interpreted by Woody Allen, has his glasses smashed by his opponents repeatedly in the course of the movie. Like Buster Keaton, "The Great Stoneface," the Allen persona has a face which is most of the time impassive. For example, in *Crimes and Misdemeanors* (1989), while his wife is making a scene, reproaching him with his lack of ambition and his professional failure, Cliff Stern, the Allen persona, does not react and, seemingly uninterested, eats an apple. The persona's emotions are hardly transmitted through his expression—he constantly looks sad or surprised—and seldom through words or gestures. Like Keaton's persona, Allen's is a fatalist. Mast asserts that it is this similar unchanging expression in both actors which emphasizes their mental activity, and which help them survive in hostile environments. As Mast puts it: "the face is a mask, a ruse, a cover for the ceaseless activity of the brain beneath." (128)

More significant, however, are Allen's similarities to Charlie Chaplin. Like Chaplin, Allen creates and plays with a persona who is unsuccessful by nature and whose humor combines pathos and slapstick: the Tramp (Chaplin) and the Little Man (Allen). Chaplin's *City Lights* (1931) is reputed to be Allen's favorite screen comedy and its ending is said to have inspired the ending scene of *Manhattan* (1979), when a close-up of the persona's face emphasizes his emotions. As Chaplin did,

Allen plays several parts in the elaboration of his films: he writes the script, directs the different stages of the filmmaking and, most often, is an actor in them. As Chaplin had his hat, his mustache, his cane and his duck-walking as signs of physical recognition, Allen has his glasses— which seem to be another screen between the screen and the spectator— and his stammering. Louis Giannetti remarks that the Tramp wearing baggy trousers and too-tight coats—as Allen's persona does—suggested insignificance and reinforced the impression of his vulnerability (301).

Chaplin and Allen also share the same view of creativity. In the same way as Allen states that there is no rational explanation for the compulsion of artistic creativity, in *Limelight* (1952), clown Calvero, interpreted by Chaplin, says before entering the stage for his final performance: "This is where I belong." As Terry, the ballerina, replies: "I thought you hated the theater", he adds: "I do. I also hate the sight of blood, but it's in my veins." This could easily apply to Allen's persona—and maybe to Allen himself—who have a paradoxical relationship with their environments and interests in life. Thus, although Allen's devotion to New York City is a well-known fact, he has Ike say in *Manhattan* that he considered the city "a metaphor for the decay of contemporary culture", justifying his ambiguous relationship with it by adding that "love is irrational." Similarly, at the end of *Annie Hall*, Alvy focusses on the irrationality of love, in a voice over:

> I-I thought of that old joke, you know, this-this-this guy goes to
> a psychiatrist and says, "Doc, uh, my brother's crazy. He thinks
> he's a chicken." And, uh, the doctor says, "Well, why don't you
> turn him in?" And the guy says, "I would, but I need the eggs."
> Well, I guess that's pretty much how how I feel about relation-
> ships. You know, they're totally irrational and crazy and absurd
> and … but, uh, I guess we keep goin' through it because, uh,
> most of us need the eggs.(Allen *Four Films* 105)

Both directors share the same pessimistic view of humanity. Thus, Neil Sinyard wrote, regarding Chaplin's *Monsieur Verdoux* (1947): "He contemplates the proposition that the insanity and injustice of the world might finally overwhelm even a decent man and turn him a monster"(42). In fact, this could apply to Judah Rosenthal, one of the main characters of Allen's *Crimes and Misdemeanors* (1989), played by actor Martin Landau, who has his lover killed because she threatens him to reveal the whole truth about their affair—among other things—to his wife.

Finally, Foster Hirsch contends that, as Chaplin had done earlier, Woody Allen set up two fictional characters, his persona in the framework of his movies, and another character that he plays in real life:

> His one regret in life is that he is not someone else. . . . As it happens, though, Woody Allen *is* someone else. He is a comic fabrication, as much a result of conscious artisanship as Chaplin's Tramp.(6–7)

Like Chaplin and Keaton, Allen's movies tackled moral issues such as the problem of uprightness and self-accomplishment. Like Allen's, Keaton's persona kept to his ideal, but was often a failure. As Allen repeatedly does, Keaton tried to dismantle the literary and social clichés about "human worth": his unheroic, unromantic persona could accomplish much in spite of his original disadvantages.

The Persona's Jewish Origins

The male persona of Woody Allen, Allen himself, has two cultural backgrounds, which may account for his quest for identity and explain for his ambivalent relationship with society. His origin is Jewish. He is very different from the people around him and can seldom adapt to his environments. But at the same time, he needs mainstream American models, as he does in *Play it Again, Sam* (1972), in which he models his behavior with women on Humphrey Bogart's, or he naturally identifies to someone else, as he does in *Zelig* (1983).

His humor, either physical or witty, has been typically Jewish from the start. If Woody Allen's humor has always been in line with Jewish tradition, this aspect has still become more important in some movies where the persona has a less physical part. However Woody Allen is in the habit of claiming his disinterest in his Jewishness and of denying the influence it had on his personality, his personal view of life, and on his works. Thus, he said to Natalie Gittelson who interviewed him for *The New York Times Magazine*, in 1979:

> It's not on my mind; it's no part of my artistic consciousness. There are certain cultural differences between Jews and non-Jews, I guess, but I think they're largely superficial. Of course, any character I play would be Jewish, just because I'm Jewish. I'm also metropolitan-oriented. I wouldn't play a farmer or an

Irish seaman. So I write about metropolitan characters who happen to be Jewish . . . (106)

However, I share the opinion of Sam Girgus who does not agree with Allen's above statement and who asserts that Allen always "manipulated the Jewish aspect of his public persona" (38). The Jewish milieux that Woody Allen stages are often presented in too caricatural a way to have been referred to naturally. Similarly, Philip Roth argues that Allen asserts his Jewishness. He distinguishes two types of Jews: the "Jewish Jew" and the "Non-Jewish Jew". While admitting that elements of both Jews can be found in Allen's persona, he nevertheless contends that Woody Allen's persona is essentially a Jewish Jew, "conscience-stricken, paranoid, defensive, victimized, moral, sensitive, and filled with denial." (22–28).

Despite the apparent influence of Jewish humor on the formation of the persona, Jewish environments and characters are not presented in a favorable light in Allen's movies. The Jewish persona is a paranoid outsider who suffers from his belonging to Jewry much more than he takes it on. Thus, in *Annie Hall*, he insists to his friend Rob that NBC reporter Tom Christie has said "Did Jew . . . ?" instead of "Did you . . . ?" He imagines Grammy Hall seeing him as a long-bearded Hassid. In *Hannah and Her Sisters*, he wants to escape his Jewishness, which does not enable him to find a meaning to his life, by adopting another religion.

The Jewish family is also problematic for Allen's persona. As already mentioned, his parents are presented as rejecting him, as they do in *Take the Money and Run* (1967), for example. His mother is possessive and interferes with his life in *Oedipus Wrecks* (1988). In *Annie Hall*, the family of the protagonist, Alvy Singer, is presented in parallel to Annie's family, through the use of a split-screen and in the framework of a Thanksgiving dinner. Whereas the Hall family is warm and welcoming, the Singer family is noisy, seems quarrelsome, and their conversation topics range from bad health to work problems. In *Stardust Memories*, Sandy Bates's Jewish fans are presented—according to the persona's standpoint—as grotesque figures, through wide-angle shots which distort their faces.

Jewish humorists have always made people laugh by conflating the flaws or at least the characteristics of their own environments. Allen goes further when he has his persona reject his Jewishness in *Hannah and Her Sisters* and the main male character of *Crimes and Misdemeanors* betray his Jewish education. Allen's negative vision of Jewry could easily be criticized. For example, in *Deconstructing Harry*, the persona clearly makes fun of and even opposes the Jewish fanaticism of his sister and brother-in-law, as if Woody Allen had wanted to hammer it in.

Self-Referential Aspects

The third important characteristic of Woody Allen's persona—that which has probably been most explored and caused the most controversy—is the seemingly self-referential aspect of some movies, such as *Stardust Memories, Husbands and Wives* (the last movie that starred Mia Farrow, in 1992) or *Deconstructing Harry*. Woody Allen always denied that he reproduced his life on screen and even that he expressed his personal ideas. Nevertheless, some elements of his movies—professional and cultural environments or events—bear so many resemblances to Woody Allen and the events of his personal life, even his childhood, that we may doubt his denials. This ambiguous aspect of Allen's movies makes the spectators doubly "voyeurs": they are watching a piece of fiction but cannot help relating it to Allen's real life.

One of the characteristics of the persona—and maybe of the director—is his egotism. As Gérard Genette wrote:

> Le paradoxe de l'egotisme est à peu près celui-ci : parler de soi, de la manière la plus indiscrète et la plus impudique, peut être le meilleur moyen de se dérober. L'egotisme est dans tous les sens du terme une parade. (157)

Woody Allen staging himself would be intended to cloud the issue and, in fact, to hide himself. Writer Mary Nichols admits that Woody Allen projects his life in his movies, but considers it part of his art:

> There is no question that Allen's movies are self-reflective. But self-reflection can mean examination of one's own art as well as indulgent projection of private vice. (xi)

Several characteristics of Woody Allen's movies encourage this self-referential vision. Woody Allen is, as the famous credit titles of his movies recall, writer of his scripts and director of his movies. Consequently, the persona introduces a reality which is necessarily sifted through his creator's perspective. Created by, and originally for Woody Allen, the persona displays the physical characteristics of his author, somewhat amplified, and might display his psychological traits, too. Moreover, Woody Allen shows people in their private life. The fact that he happens to be the narrator of stories in which he is an actor reinforces the impression of reality. Thus, in *Annie Hall* and *Radio Days* (1986), the audience may think that he is telling his own story.

Allen stages his movies in his own professional and social environments. The persona moves in Manhattan, as Woody Allen does. He is most of the time an intellectual and even a filmmaker. The actors he hires are most of the time his friends and several actresses who played in his movies have been his wife (Louise Lasser) or his real life companions (Diane Keaton and Mia Farrow). He made *Annie Hall* after his split with Diane Keaton and Alvy Singer arguably relives the reasons for this split.

It is well acknowledged that Woody Allen was under psychoanalysis for over thirty-five years. The persona too is generally a neurotic whose caustic comments about psychoanalysts—although he often needs their help—might also be addresses to Allen's own psychoanalysts who have not succeeded in helping him get rid of his neuroses after so long a time. Woody Allen's schlemiel is a reversal of the traditional American, specifically Hollywoodian, movie hero, a kind of New York David against Hollywood Goliath. The traditional Hollywoodian hero epitomized masculinity at its extreme: he was strong, a protector of women. On the contrary, when the persona plays the heroes, it is in a burlesque tone, as he does in *Bananas* (1969). Woody Allen's persona exhibits allegedly "feminine" characteristics: for example, he speaks in a high-pitched voice and is often a coward. Thus, in *Manhattan*, Jill (played by Meryl Streep), Ike's ex-wife who has left him and has turned a lesbian, wrote in her book that he cried each time he saw *Gone with the Wind* (1939).

Like Woody Allen, who makes movies but tries to find anonymity, his persona simultaneously seeks fame and wants to escape it. This is true in *Annie Hall, Stardust Memories, Zelig,* and *Hannah and Her Sisters*. While ostensibly reclusive, he often looks self-centered and even narcissistic. He is so obsessed with his own problems that he does not get much interested in others. His apparent inferiority complex might, in fact, conceal a strong superiority complex. In *Stardust Memories*, when someone tells him "You've been accused of being narcissistic", he replies: "Well, actually, the Greek god I would identify with is not Narcissus but Zeus." However this opinion has to be tempered. In *Zelig,* for example, which is a movie which deals with the problem of "personality", he is not narcissistic since he becomes all those he approaches. Woody Allen confines himself to his personal universe without intending to extend it to the world.

Allen himself regrets that people consider some of his movies as exclusively autobiographical. Playing the role of the persona seems to have become a burden to him. In an interview to *The New York Times Magazine*, he insists that he would have prefered not to play in *Deconstructing Harry*:

> With my latest movie, *Deconstructing Harry*, which I wanted to call "The Meanest Man in the World", I wrote it, and I would have hoped someone else would have played the lead role. It's boring for me to play it all the time. It's more fun to direct now and then and not have to shave every day. But I couldn't get anybody else. I was my last choice. Until three weeks before we shot, I was sweating to get somebody else and couldn't do it. I offered it to a half-dozen people and could not work it out for some reason or another with them, and so finally I did it. . . . And there is no question: they'll think I am the character. But they think that in everything I do. I don't care. That is one of the curses or the blessings of what I do. That is why they come or why they stay away." (Hirschberg *New York Times,* 96)

The Persona's Major Characteristics

The male persona does not involve himself in events most of the time. Instead he lets himself be led into them. He always keeps at some distance from what happens to him and around him, which enables him to keep an objective view. Basically, he is an outsider who often struggles for acceptance into mainstream America. However we must recognize that he is often someone who has already been accepted into his environments, as he is often professionally successful. His quest is not really a quest for identity but rather the quest of a victim of angst who seeks to find a meaning to his life. The persona's desire to be accepted, his need for reassurance, is a recurrent motif in American mass entertainment. Thus, Werner Sollors asserts that: "In America, casting oneself as an outsider may in fact be considered a dominant cultural trait" (31).

The persona's lack of self-confidence, the self-effacing attitude that he generally adopts, leads him to believe that he has no impact on his environment. Thus Marguerite Duras wrote about him:

> Il est seulement là où il est. Autour de lui, rien ne bouge, les choses restent différentes, elles ne partent pas avec lui, il ne modifie rien. New York autour de lui est pareil. Il traverse New York et New York est pareil. (18)

This aspect of the character can be explained by the fact that Woody Allen's movies, which start *in media res*, are slices of life and not initiatory journeys. However we cannot fully agree with Duras's statement for, through his role as a mentor, for example, the persona brings people to change.

Paradoxically, although the persona generally moves in a restricted space—almost exclusively Manhattan because Allen generally limits himself to Manhattan—and is representative of a certain contemporary type of character, we can consider the persona a universal character. He is a regular guy—the guy next door—with "normal" concerns which range from the problems or conflicts of a well-defined part of contemporary society and transcend it to questioning the meaning of life. He does not experience extraordinary events, as Hollywood's male characters often do.

The Persona's Relationship to the Audience

The persona is a character whom spectators can at least partly identify with. As already said, he is often an ordinary man with the same problems as regular people. At least until the most recent films, the persona aroused affection in the audience. Spectators shared his anxieties and tended to take sides with him. For instance, they might have resented the fact Halley chooses Lester and not the person in *Crimes and Misdemeanors*. However we can think that at least a part of this potential identification is due to the fact that the persona is embodied by successful director Woody Allen, a man who achieved great success in spite of initial physical and social disadvantages. The audience cannot identify with the persona when the latter is presented as too "inferior" to the audience, as he might be in *Deconstructing Harry*, for example.

The relationship Woody Allen has with his audience is ambiguous, a combination of identification and rejection. He happens to identify his persona with moviegoers by staging him as a spectator, as he does in *Husbands and Wives*. On the other hand, he could be reproached with presenting the audience in a rather contemptuous manner, as he did in *Stardust Memories*, which may be seen as a settling of scores. *In Stardust Memories*, Allen seems to be anticipating on screen—and generating—the reaction triggered by the movie in the audience. He has repeatedly said that he was striving to achieve a masterpiece, which, according to him, runs counter to the public's demands.

Therefore, Allen has never concealed his antipathy for the Hollywoodian cinema and its audience. Every time this cinema is mentioned in his movies, it is in a caricatural manner. It is presented not as an art but as a business. Woody Allen gives no quarter except for the old movies he likes. Thus *Everybody says I Love You* is a musical, which reminds us of the movies dating back to the great epoch of American musicals, such as the movies in which Fred Astaire and Gingers Rogers played and danced. However, Hollywood movies are often presented in an unfavorable light. In *The Purple Rose of Cairo*, in which Woody pays homage to movies from the 30s, it is the Hollywoodian business which is attacked. The team of the film-within-the-film—entitled *The Purple Rose of Cairo* too—is entirely preoccupied with the possible financial impact of Tom Baxter's desertion. Hearing Tom Baxter exclaim "I want a place to hide", it is difficult not to think of Woody Allen trying to escape journalists and other groupies, as he does in *Stardust Memories*. When Tom says a bit later: "I want to live. I want to be free to make my own choices," it is also difficult not to think of the director frustrated by the constraints imposed on him.

Therefore, Tom seems to be expressing the director's aspirations, his opinion about life, but also his opinion about his professional environment and about the audience as well:

> TOM: So that's what popcorn tastes like. I've been watching people eat it for all those performances. When they rattle those bags, though, that's, uh ...
> CECILIA: That's not ... ?
> TOM: ... kind of annoying.

Tom might also be expressing the director's self-confidence and hypersensitivity when he reacts, stammering, to what Cecilia has just told him about his part in the movie, annoyed with being questioned: "You don't—You don't think I'm the main character?" Foster Hirsch thinks that Woody Allen is in fact Allan Konigsberg's public character: ". . . he is playing himself or at least playing on the public image of himself that he shrewdly has orchestrated." (363) Woody Allen's persona shares some characteristics of Woody Allen, who is not the real Allan Konigsberg.

The persona has taken such a hypertrophied place that even where it is not Woody Allen who interprets it, spectators cannot help seeking it . . . and can generally find it. This desire is parodied in *Everybody Says I Love You*, where all male characters, young and older, gesticulate exactly in the same manner as the persona does, are dressed with the same kind of clothes, and all of them have similar behaviors as regards women: they let themselves be led. There seems to be a kind of multiplication, a scattering of the characteristics of the persona into the other male characters, a multiple reflection of his personality on them. This constitutes a reversal of *Sleeper* (1973), in which the disguised persona tried to hide among robots all alike, or even of *Zelig*. It looks as if the aging Woody Allen were reproducing and multiplying the persona, which he will be soon unable to play. To give birth to "clones" to his persona might be a means to prevent him from dying—an admission of the filmmaker's fear of death.

Works Cited

Allen, Woody. *Four Films of Woody Allen*. New York: Random House, 1982.

Björkman, Stig. *Woody Allen on Woody Allen: In Conversation with Stig Björkman*. London: Faber and Faber, 1994.

Duras, Marguerite. "Les Yeux Vents." *Les Cahiers du Cinema*. 1997.

Genette, Gerard, *Figures II*. Paris: Editions de Sevil, 1969.

Gianetti, Louis. *Understanding Movies*. Englewood Cliffs, NJ: Prentice Hall, 1990.

Girgus, Sam. *The Films of Woody Allen*. New York: St Martin's Press. 1982.

Gittleson, Natalie. "The Maturing of Woody Allen." *The New York Times Magazine*, April 22, 1979.

Hirsch, Foster. *Love, Sex, Death and the Meaning of Life: The Films of Woody Allen*. New York: Limelight Editions, 1990.

Hirshchberg, Lynn. "Woody Allen, Martin Scorcese." *The New York Times Magazine*, November 16, 1997.

Mast, Gerald. *The Comic Mind: Comedy and the Movies*. Chicago: University of Chicago Press, 1979.

Nichols, Mary. *Reconstructing Woody: Art, Love, and Life in the Films of Woody Allen*. Lanham, MD: Rowan and Littlefield, 1998.

Roth, Philip. "Imagining Jews." *The New York Review of Books*, October 1974.

Sinyard, Neil. *Directors: The All-Time Greats*. London: Columbus Books, 1985.

Sollors, Werner. *Beyond Ethnicity: Consent and Dissent in American Culture*. New York: Oxford University Press, 1986.

Woody Allen: An American Comedy. Films for the Humanities. Princeton, New Jersey, 1977.

"Just a Laugh Machine"
Don't Drink the Water on Stage and Screen

WILLIAM HUTCHINGS

Starting with Mark Twain's *Innocents Abroad* (1869) and continuing at least through *National Lampoon's European Vacation* (1985), the American tourist abroad has become as much a stock comic figure as the miser, the misanthrope, the jealous elderly husband, and the *miles gloriosus* (braggart soldier) were centuries ago. Easily recognizable in their garish attire and (in the twentieth century) with ever-present cameras hanging around their necks, they are typically bewildered by the sheer Otherness of There: customs that are "foreign" in every sense of the word, foods that are unpalatably unlike the Familiar, and water that, coming unfluoridated and perhaps not from a tap, can wreak havoc on the digestive tract. Daniel J. Boorstin, writing in *The Image* (1961), brilliantly characterized the change "from traveler to tourist," the latter having his experience made safe and comfortable (as "authentic" travel was not) by guidebooks and travelers checks, packaged tours and prefabricated "pseudo-events"; several years earlier, the tourist's portrait had been sketched by renowned cartoonist Rube Goldberg in his satirical *Guide to Europe*. Two quintessentially "touristy" phrases provided the titles of film comedies that were both released in 1969: *If It's Tuesday This Must Be Belgium* (directed by Mel Stuart; remade for television in 1987), and *Don't Drink the Water* (directed by Howard Morris). The latter had been adapted from the long-running Broadway play that was Woody Allen's first full-length work for the stage, which opened at the Morosco Theatre on November 16, 1966; when it was remade for television in 1994, it was directed by Woody Allen himself, who also starred in this later version (unlike the previous two) and wrote its substantially revised teleplay. Allen's Broadway debut was a deftly written cold war comedy that, despite its rather formulaic plot and its stock characterization of American innocents abroad, had not only enough of its then-young author's idiosyncratic wit to please its audiences but also introduced a number of themes that would later become characteristically his own.

Set in "the American embassy in a small, Iron Curtain country somewhere in Eastern Europe" (5), *Don't Drink the Water* focuses on the plight of the Hollander family, American tourists who take refuge there after having been mistaken for spies by the communists. On their first journey abroad, Walter and Marion Hollander and their twenty-one-year-old daughter Susan are stock comic tourists who have innocently and ignorantly precipitated an international incident: the father has been caught taking photographs along the perimeter of a missile base, not realizing that snapshots of a site protected by armed guards, attack dogs, and barbed wire should not be included among his souvenirs. The mother compulsively cleans and waxes the embassy during their two-week stay there, and she serves as a comic foil who is often berated by her husband and blamed for their being there (her brother had suggested the trip instead of the family's usual excursion from their home in Newark to the New Jersey shore). The daughter is, predictably, a standard romantic ingenue, paired with Axel Magee, who is the son of the Ambassador. His father, seen briefly in the opening scene, returns to the United States to pursue his gubernatorial ambitions, leaving his assistant Kilroy—described as "a punctilious rat" in the stage directions (7)—and Axel in charge. When the Hollanders arrive at the embassy with the photographs, it is soon surrounded by angry demonstrators and encircled by machine-gun-carrying communist guards; their leader, Krojack, the head of the secret police, angrily comes on stage to demand that the spies be turned over.[1] The resolution of the crisis involves a number of standard (though deftly handled) elements of farce, including a ticking time-bomb, gunshots both on- and offstage, disguises, mistaken identities, a ridiculously elaborate escape plan, and comic alarums of various kinds. "It was just a laugh machine," as Woody Allen himself described it (quoted in Lax, *Biography*, 238).

Alongside the rather stock comic figures of the Hollanders, whose predicament drives the main plot, the play's narrator, Father Drobney, introduces Woody Allen's more idiosyncratic, often theologically or existentially-based humor. This "tall, emaciated, [and] cassocked" but congregationless priest in a "Communist country [where] of four million inhabitants, 3,975,000 are atheists, and about 24,000 are agnostics—and the other thousand are Jewish" (6) has found at the American embassy not only a refuge but practically a permanent abode, having remained there for six years since fleeing Communist authorities who intended to kill him. At that time, he faced a life-defining and faith-testing decision:

> My choice was simple. I could remain here in the safety of [the] embassy, or I could go outside and attempt the biggest mass conversion in history. I decided to stay and I've been hiding upstairs ever since. (7)

At this moment of crucial existential choice—a moment that is virtually identical to the one at which in centuries past countless saints and martyrs, facing persecution, were forever defined in the affirmation of their faith for the glory of their God—Father Drobney opted for security, expediency, and personal comfort. In doing so, he defined his values as surely (and as comically) as Falstaff on the battlefield in *Henry IV, Part One*: "Give me life; which, if I can save, so; if not, honor comes unlooked for" (V.iii.59–61). No martyr-in-the-making here, he lives in an even more unheroic age than Falstaff did; though he could readily escape, he prefers not to, claiming instead a "duty to return one day and lead my people once again" (28). With no congregation to serve and no useful function in the secular embassy, Father Drobney passes the time practicing magic tricks—the devalued counterpart of miracles—but even these fail when he finally gains a (literally) captive audience, the Hollanders. Although Marion considers his magic a "wonderful hobby" (28) and asks if he can walk on water, the illusions of this "tricky priest" (30) somehow never work out: his card tricks consistently fail, the rabbit that he would produce from a cylinder has been purloined by the chef for an entree, and the straitjacket that he allows himself to be placed into proves far more inescapable than he expected. As the play's narrator, however, he addresses the audience directly (as no other characters in the play do) and effectively handles the exposition of characters and scenes.

The play's developing love interest between Susan Hollander and Axel Magee follows the age-old formula of romantic comedy, though there is also a twist that would later become one of the most readily identifiable traits of Woody Allen's films. As in the traditional "new comedy" plot dating back to the ancient Roman playwright Plautus, boy meets girl, they fall in love, there is a problem (typically, as here, the objections of the father), the problem is overcome, and the young couple gets mar-

ried, supposedly then to live happily ever after. Unlike the typical romantic male lead, however, Axel Magee is incompetent at his job, baffled by
what's going on around him, hopelessly naive, and physically inept; in
short, he is the prototypical Woody Allen protagonist, often played by
Woody Allen himself—though on Broadway the role was performed by
Tony Roberts (who himself appeared in many of Allen's later films, often
in suave contrast to Allen's character). With blithely undiplomatic can-
dor, Axel freely admits to Krojack that Americans engage in spying, thus
inadvertently implicating the Hollanders as secret agents and endanger-
ing them even further; the audience soon understands why he has been
unable to hold a job at other embassies for longer than six months and
was "recalled" (removed or evicted) from all of Africa as well as Japan
and the Soviet Union (9). As a suitor, Axel is almost equally inept: when
he first tries to kiss Susan, he clumsily falls through a doorway; when he
suggests a romantic skiing vacation together, he reminisces about having
broken his pelvis on the slopes (41). Yet it is precisely *because* of Axel's
imperfections that Susan finds him attractive—in marked contrast to her
all-too-perfect fiancé Donald, the successful lawyer whom her father is
especially eager for her to marry when they return home. Like countless
fathers in traditional comedies throughout the centuries, Walter Hollander dominates his wife, his son at home in New Jersey (to whom he
writes letters of instruction daily), and especially his daughter, even as he
acknowledges that

> It's . . . her own life. I just want her to do the right thing, that's
> all. . . . So, what I tell her is the right thing. . . . This [Axel] is the
> worst prospect she's ever had. I like even the draft dodger she
> was going with better because he at least was a success—he
> beat the draft—something! . . . Where does happy come into it?
> I'm talking about marriage! When you get married you give up
> happiness! All of a sudden Donald can't make her happy? He's
> an attorney—he has court cases, he fills out briefs, there's mort-
> gages, there's litigation—it's romantic. (51-52)

As usual, the central conflict is not only between generations but
also between values of love and money. The variation here is that the father's choice is also, as Susan admits, "bright and *very* handsome"
(40)—the qualities of the standard male romantic lead, to whom the father is usually (for whatever reason) opposed. Axel, however, is, as Walter indicates *and as the audience sees for itself,* "what we used to call in

the pool room, a loser" when judged by traditional standards of professional, intellectual, or physical competence (52). Strategically, Donald remains unseen in the play, so that a specific contrast cannot be made—making it considerably easier to establish a comic world in which "loser takes all."

Although *Don't Drink the Water* follows the structural conventions of romantic comedy in its structure and incoroporates many forms of farce, some surprising sources and parallels for it have been acknowledged by Woody Allen himself. In his conversations with Eric Lax, the playwright disclosed that

> When I get an idea for a play, I think to myself 'What does this most closely resemble that was successful?' *Don't Drink the Water* is based on the premise of a whole family living together and getting on each other's nerves, like [George S.] Kaufman's *You Can't Take It With You*. The play is based on that source of comedy and the structure of [John Patrick's] *Teahouse of the August Moon*. Nobody has pointed out the similarity, but it's true. (209)

Unless the definition of "family" is broadened to include Father Drobney and members of the embassy staff (i.e., all who share the embassy house), however, the link to Kaufman's work seems rather tenuous. The Hollanders' interactions and ongoing mutual husband-and-wife recriminations, while comical, are less important than their relationships with "outsiders," and the play's most memorable Kaufmanesque eccentrics are Father Drobney, Axel, Kilroy, and the embassy's chef. While *Teahouse of the August Moon* opens with direct address to the audience by Sakini and deals with the relationship between Americans abroad (American Marines in Okinawa after World War II), an equally plausible parallel for *Don't Drink the Water* could be found in the various Alfred Hitchcock films in which innocent civilians are caught up in espionage or other international intrigue (e.g., *The 39 Steps*, *North by Northwest*, *The Man Who Knew Too Much*). The play was finished in early 1966 when Allen was in London for the filming of the James Bond travesty *Casino Royale*, though it went through substantial revisions (including the addition of Father Drobney as narrator) during its pre-Broadway run in Philadelphia and Boston.[2] The role of Walter Hollander was conceived for actor Lou Jacobi, whom Allen's biographer Eric Lax describes as "the mustachioed, sad-eyed personification of the self-made Jewish character" (*Biography*, 234); the playwright objected to producer David Merrick's choice of Vivian Vance, who played Ethel Mertz in television's *I Love Lucy* series, for the role of Marion Hollander, feeling that she was not ethnic enough (she was replaced prior to the Broadway opening by Kay Medford). The extent to which an individual production is or is not particularly ethnic remains of course a matter of directorial choice.

A more surprising production issue involves the onstage gunshots during the play's second act. Like Joe Orton's *What the Butler Saw* (posthumously produced in 1969) but unlike most traditional farces, *Don't Drink the Water* contains gunshots which hit their targets: Kilroy is accidentally shot in the leg by Walter at the end of act 2 scene 2 (68), as is Ambassador Magee at the end of act 2 scene 3 (74), who spends the final scene in a wheelchair pushed by Axel. Although the shots allow Walter to "feel toughened up [for his escape] . . . now that [he has] drawn blood" (75), and although on a symbolic level it is apropos that the two most "punctilious" representatives of governmental authority are those who suffer the most during the mayhem that farce requires, the presence of actual physical wounds undermines the comic tone of the play and dispels the resilience that victims of comic violence typically display.

With a successful Broadway run of eighteen months despite mixed reviews, *Don't Drink the Water* was a natural candidate for a film adaptation, though the playwright himself was not involved in the project. Produced by Jack Rollins and Charles H. Joffe and directed by Howard Morris from a script by R. S. Allen and Harvey Bullock, the film version was primarily a "star vehicle" for comedian Jackie Gleason, whom Woody Allen had long admired but whom he considered wrong for the part (Lax, *Biography*, 234); the role of Marion is played by Estelle Parsons. Not confined to the single stage set of the embassy, the film successfully "opens out" the play to include scenes at the airport, car chases through the city (during which, predictably, a fruit vendor's cart gets smashed on two separate occasions), and a lengthy opening sequence before the titles showing the Hollanders at home in New Jersey preparing for their trip—getting shots, ordering passports, buying clothes, packing loads of toilet paper and pills, boarding their dog, and departing at the airport. The film also provides a more plausible reason for the Hollanders' presence in an unlikely tourist venue like Vulgaria (a name that is not used in the play): their flight into Athens gets hijacked and lands at the airport at or near the communists' military installation, which Walter photographs during a brief interval when passengers are allowed off the plane. When chased by the local troops, the Hollanders run to the American-flag-bearing diplomatic limousine that is parked on the tarmac after bringing Ambassador Magee to the airport for his flight back to the United States. Scenes within the embassy are reasonably consistent with those in the play, providing ample opportunities for Gleason's trademark "slow burn" exasperation and sarcastically droll asides, but some motifs have been enhanced with sight gags, such as Kilroy's arm being in a sling from a fall (unseen) on Mrs. Hollander's perpetually waxed floors. Father Drobney's narration has been cut out entirely, and topical references to Richard Nixon and his vice president, Spiro Agnew, have been added, as has a lengthy sequence in which a precisely scheduled and staged "spontaneous" demonstration (directed by Krojack) is shown outside the embassy.

In another added plot development, Walter nearly touches off another international incident by insulting the visiting Sultan of Bashir, who expresses an interest in adding Susan to his harem. She dresses as a boy during the escape (which is arranged by a CIA agent who is not in the play); when she is seen by the chef kissing Axel while in disguise, it prompts a direct-into-the-camera joke from the chef about Axel's presumed sexual orientation: "That's life in the State Department for you." Ambassador Magee announces a scheme for the Hollanders to spend thirty days in jail before his intervention securing their release, but Walter locks Krojack and the Ambassador together in a closet and effects the family's escape in an elaborate sequence that involves a commandeered secret police van, a school bus, a horse-drawn load of hay, a biplane, and the Sultan of Bashir's Rolls Royce as well as his (and his wives') clothing—all to a musical soundtrack that emphasizes the scene's parodic similarity to the derring-do on the television series *Mission: Impossible*, which had had its debut in 1966. The gunshots that wound Kilroy and the Ambassador in the stage version have been omitted in the film, although Gleason does a brief James Cagney impersonation shortly after being given the gun (the famously pugnacious and cocksure line "You dirty rat!"). Among all the changes between the stage and screen versions, however, naming the country Vulgaria may have been the most prescient: Walter Hollander is certainly not the last Woody Allen character to find himself "besieged by Vulgarians," as viewers of *Stardust Memories*, *Deconstructing Harry*, and *Celebrity* well know.

The romantic relationship between Susan and Axel also undergoes quite a transformation in the transition from stage to screen, adhering more closely to the conventions of "new comedy" in the film. As played by the tall and blond Ted Bessell (who looks—and some would add acts—disconcertingly like former Vice President Dan Quayle), Axel is much more the traditional male romantic lead than he seems to be in the play's script. Though still rather dimwitted and naive, he is decidedly more handsome than his rival Donald, who is seen in the pre-title sequence at the airport; he is unctuously solicitous as he escorts Susan to the plane and is nerdily attired in an ill-fitting business suit, horn-rimmed glasses, and a pork-pie hat—all of which were especially egregious violations of the standards for men's fashions (especially young men's fashions) in the late 1960's. Susan, played by Joan Delaney, is far less demure than she seems in the play. As a young woman attuned to the then-blossoming "sexual revolution," she responds affirmatively and even aggressively to Axel's advances, and when he accidentally discloses that the embassy has a secret passageway linking her bedroom to his, she is ready and even eager to explore (this scene replaces the one in the play in which he clumsily falls through an open doorway). She is seen by her father in a passionate embrace with Axel outdoors at the embassy, and she is unabashed when her father finds her coming out of Axel's room—as well as when, just before departing the embassy, Walter discovers the secret passageway linking their bedrooms and remarks (rather futilely) that they are getting away "just in time." In fact, the couple remains behind in Vulgaria at the end of the movie as her parents escape in the biplane, and they are married (as in the play) by Father Drobney. The film's final image is a close-up of a large red flower that the new bride is carrying—an affirmation not only of "flower power" (the then-popular slogan) but also of love and fertility, that hardy perennial comic theme.

When *Don't Drink the Water* was produced as a television movie in 1994, with Woody Allen as its director, screenplay adapter, and star, the effects of his quarter century of experience as an actor, writer, and director became readily apparent.[3] This version remains much more faithful to the original play, as one would expect: the Iron Curtain country remains unnamed, and almost all of the action takes place inside the embassy or on its grounds; there is no secret passageway between bedrooms (or if there is, it remains a secret), Donald the fiancé remains unseen (though he is now a dermatologist rather than a lawyer), and the Hollanders' escape takes place as Walter and Marion disguise themselves as two of the emir's wives; no multi-vehicle escape is seen, no car chases occur, and no biplane in sight. The Hollanders' presence behind the iron curtain is explained by their being part of a tour group (unlikely though that was in the late 1960's), and they seek refuge at the embassy rather than the airport. Although an expository narrative is used in the film, it is not delivered by Father Drobney. Instead, following a title sequence in the plain white-on-black style used in many of Allen's films, a series of newsreel-style scenes from the mid-1960's provides historical context that would obviously have been unneeded when the play was first produced and when the previous movie version was made. The sequence gains authenticity in that it is narrated by Ed Herlihy, a well known announcer and news-reader at that time. The time bomb episode is much more brief than in the previous film, and there is not an explosion following it as there is in the play—in large part, presumably, because of the reaction that such an event would bring from the Marine security guards who are prominently visible at their posts in the embassy during several scenes. Notwithstanding their presence, however, Walter's gunshots *are* fired in the movie, hitting the "emir's assistant" (rather than Kilroy) in the foot and the Ambassador in the arm, although both wounds are apparently quite minor. Viewers see the emir's assistant fall when he is shot on a stairway, but the Ambassador's wounding occurs off-camera when he is outside the embassy doors and (quite implausibly) elicits no reaction from the security staff. During the film's final scene, the voiceover narrative reveals that Axel left the diplomatic service after marrying Susan; he is last seen working for his father-in-law as a caterer in New Jersey, sculpting wedding reception statuettes of a bride and groom out of chopped liver.

The cast of the 1994 version was extraordinarily stellar for a television movie, although many were playing their already well-established types. In his first major television performance since a "Woody Allen Special" for Kraft Music Hall in 1969 (O'Connor), Woody Allen himself plays Walter Hollander— a role for which he would have been much too young when he wrote it— with the range of mannerisms and quirks that has become popularly associated with his various comic personae: anxiety, helplessness, neurosis, talky desperation, alleged physical maladies (real or imagined), and fetishism. A scene added to the teleplay shows Walter phoning home to ask that he be sent a piece of gray flannel from underneath his pillow, claiming that it helps him fall asleep when he puts its corner in his mouth. Although the family's Jewishness is referred to only rather indirectly (in a question about rabbis during a discussion of marriage in the final minutes of the film), their *general* ethnicity is emphasized more than in the earlier film, particularly in the characters of Marion (played by Julie Kavner) and Susan (played by Mayim Bialik). To his role of Axel Magee, Michael J. Fox brings much of the preppiness and geniality that was associated with his character Alex Keaton on the long-running television series *Family Ties*; with such a plausible romantic lead playing the part, the character's general ineptitude was played down in contrast to the more typical "Woody Allen" character that he is in the original play. As Kilroy, Edward Hermann provided an effective older, wiser, and taller foil for Fox in running the embassy, and Dom DeLuise brought to the role of Father Drobney the comic brashness, loudness, and exuberance that are his trademarks. Although the role of Krojack is considerably diminished in the teleplay (he neither enters the embassy as in the play nor choreographs the demonstration as in the film), Vit Horejs is a look-alike for his character's almost-namesake Kojak, the bald detective lieutenant played by Telly Savalas in the CBS television series that ran from 1973 through 1978; the scenes in the Secret Police headquarters cleverly parody those in the New York police station in which the long-popular series was set.

At least prior to the making of the television movie in 1994, with its substantial rewrites and its extraordinary cast, Woody Allen's own assessments of the play have been surprisingly harsh. Citing a film by Harold Mantell entitled *Woody Allen: An American Comedy*, Maurice Yacowar claims that Allen "rejects this early dramatic effort as 'a really terrible play,' just a series of funny jokes strung together" (49–50). Similarly, during one of the interviews given Eric Lax for the 1991 biography, Allen remarked that

> Laughs are what the thing floated on. It had nothing else going for it but that. Yet I know it was full of weaknesses of the worst kind. I was just jumping into the water to get my feet wet. I haven't read the play in years. It's probably dreadful beyond words—but full of funny lines. (*Biography*, 238)

Nevertheless, his willingness to rewrite it, direct it, and star in it only three years later suggests that his opinion of it was—or at least became—considerably less severe; the television version was reportedly filmed in only three weeks (O'Connor). Although *Don't Drink the Water* obviously lacks the complexity of characterization and the degree of sophistication that would characterize his later works, it portends many of the comic directions that they would take. When assessed among other young playwrights' first efforts, or when placed alongside other Broadway comedies that were roughly contemporaneous with it (e.g., Neil Simon's *Star Spangled Girl*, which also opened on Broadway in 1966), or when considered within the context of the quite formulaic tradition of

"Americans-abroad" comedies, *Don't Drink the Water* may indeed be "just a laugh machine" and one of Woody Allen's minor works, but it is also one that holds up surprisingly well today.

Notes

[1]Krojack's entrance is one of many examples of dramatic license in the play. At an actual United States Embassy, no matter what its size or what the country, whether in the 1960s or now, Krojack would not have gotten past its detachment of Marine security guards, who would be manning both its gate house and, inside the embassy, the reception area known as Post One. In the 1994 television movie, however, these oversights were corrected, and Marine security guards are prominent in a number of scenes both inside and outside the embassy. I am grateful to former Marine Security Guard Staff Sergeant Brad Byerley for providing me with details of embassy protocol.

[2]For a detailed account of the production travails and cast changes that preceded the Broadway opening, see Eric Lax, *On Being Funny: Woody Allen and Comedy* (New York: Charterhouse, 1975), 209–213 and Lax, *Woody Allen: A Biography* (New York: Knopf, 1991), 232–238.

[3]I am grateful to Marcus Lusk of The Optic Nerve in Birmingham, Alabama for initial information on the television version of *Don't Drink the Water*, and to Carol Williams for providing me with a videotape of it from her personal collection.

Bibliography

Allen, Woody. *Don't Drink the Water*. New York: Samuel French, 1967.
———. *Don't Drink the Water.* Adapted and dir. Woody Allen. Prod. Robert Greenhut. With Woody Allen and Michael J. Fox. ABC Sunday Night Movie. ABC. 18 December 1994.
———. *Don't Drink the Water.* Adapted R. S. Allen and Harvey Bullock. Dir. Howard Morris. Prod. Jack Rollins and Charles H. Joffe. With Jackie Gleason and Estelle Parsons. Avco Embassy Pictures, 1969.
Boorstin, Daniel J. "From Traveler to Tourist: The Lost Art of Travel." *The Image: A Guide to Pseudo-Events in America.* New York: Random-Vintage, 1992.
Goldberg, Rube. *Rube Goldberg's Guide to Europe.* New York: Vanguard, 1954.
If It's Tuesday, This Must Be Belgium. Writ. David Shaw. Dir. Mel Stewart. Prod. Stan Marguiles. With Suzanne Pleshette and Ian Mac-

Shane. United Artists, 1969.

Kaufman, George S. and Moss Hart. *You Can't Take It With You.* 1936. New York: Dramatists Play Service, 1964.

Lax, Eric. *On Being Funny: Woody Allen and Comedy.* New York: Charterhouse, 1975.

———. *Woody Allen: A Biography.* New York: Knopf, 1991.

National Lampoon's European Vacation. Writ. John Hughes and Robert Klane. Dir. Amy Heckerling. Prod. Matty Simmons. With Chevy Chase and Beverly D'Angelo. Warner Brothers, 1985.

O'Connor, John J. "TV Weekend: Woody Allen Revisits a Venue of Long Ago." *New York Times* 16 Dec. 1994. D22.

Patrick, John. *The Teahouse of the August Moon.* Rev. ed. New York: Samuel French, 1957.

Twain, Mark. *The Innocents Abroad, Or The New Pilgrim's Progress.* 1869. New York: NAL-Signet, 1982.

Yacowar, Maurice. *Loser Take All: The Comic Art of Woody Allen.* New expanded edition. New York: Continuum, 1991.

The Nebbish King
Spiritual Renewal in Woody Allen's *Manhattan*

LEE FALLON

Given Woody Allen's deliberate and apposite selection of the music for his films, one wonders at his omission of the Maurice Chevalier classic "Thank Heaven for Little Girls" for *Manhattan,* the 1979 hymn to a decaying city and a budding girl. But lest this musing be misconstrued as a cheap shot informed by the *auteur*'s domestic vicissitudes, it should at once be said that the purpose here is not to exploit the broadly supposed Pygmalion persona of the man, but rather to consider the urban malaise that necessitates such May-December dalliance in Allen's Unreal City as a modern avatar of the anthropological phenomenon of the Fisher King. In light of this, it is not sexual peccadillo, but spiritual rejuvenation, that is at issue in Manhattan.

As the film opens, Ike is trying to find the right tone with which to begin his novel, which, of course, is also Allen's attempt to establish the worldview of his protagonist. In one of his false starts, or at least one of the beginnings Ike rejects, he describes Manhattan as a metaphor for the decay of civilization. He quickly dismisses this, not because he disagrees with it, but because such a concept would be too morbid to sell books. Though the tone he finally settles on suggests a brash, romantic swagger, a few moments of familiarity with the character who boasts that he "was as tough and romantic as the city he loved," and that "behind his black-rimmed glasses was the coiled sexual power of a jungle cat," show us instead a wounded man in crisis, one whose sexual powers have been cast into doubt by his second ex-wife who has left him for another woman. Granting that the Woody Allen persona is indeed the king of Manhattan (he punctuates his favored beginning with the assertion: "New York was *his* town, and it always would be), his New York story is a kind of quest, one whose grail is the rejuvenation of faith in humanity, and one that requires a pure hero to effect this restoration of hope to the king and land.

The connections between Manhattan and the legend of the Fisher King become clearer in light of Jessie Weston's influential work on the Grail Myth, *From Ritual to Romance*. She observes that there exists "a close connection between the vitality of a certain King, and the prosperity of his kingdom; the forces of the ruler being weakened or destroyed by wound, sickness, old age, or death, the land becomes Waste, and the task of the hero is that of restoration" (21). Correspondingly, the wound in *Manhattan* is sexual humiliation by Jill, the Waste is the spiritually bankrupt landscape of Allen's "dying city," and the hero is, with characteristic Allen irony, the ingenue with the voice Ike compares to the mouse in the Tom and Jerry cartoons.

The general spiritual lassitude of Allen protagonists in a number of his films assumes a more specific psychic wound in *Manhattan*. Weston notes that the Fisher King's wound was in some versions of the Grail Quest a result of his marriage to an unbeliever: "the Fisher King . . . is ensnared by the beauty of the daughter of the Pagan King of Norway . . . he baptizes her, though she is still an unbeliever at heart, and makes her his wife, thus drawing the wrath of Heaven upon himself" (20). Ike, too, acts against his better judgement in marrying Jill. When he expresses his continuing bafflement over her preferring a woman to him, Jill replies "you knew my history when you married me." Ike replies "Yeah, my analyst told me it was insane, but you were so beautiful, I got another analyst." He "baptizes" Jill into heterosexual union, conceiving a child with her, despite her lingering doubts about sex with men; she is still an unbeliever at heart. He then reaps the consequences of his rash decision, a devastating blow to his sexual potency.

Mary, then, after Ike has confessed this, is right when she says it is perfectly understandable that Ike would embrace Tracy, a symbol of youthful innocence: "I think it accounts for the little girl." Though she guesses wrong that Ike does so because Tracy is "no threat whatsoever" to his ego. Ike loves Tracy because she restores his faith in people, even if that faith is tenuous and liable to give way beneath the temptation of another pagan princess, the emotionally antiseptic, tediously intellectual Mary, whose repeated insistence that she is "brilliant and beautiful" recalls the narcissism of which Jill accuses Ike in her book. Their alliance yields naught but confusion, and Ike, the wounded Nebbish King of New

York, must continue to wait for renewal in the aesthetically vibrant but spiritually bankrupt Waste of Manhattan.

The land the Allen protagonist rules over is infertile, in that it no longer breeds faith and contentment. For all the oft-noted beauty Allen and cinematographer Gordon Willis achieve in *Manhattan*'s signature shot of the Queensborough Bridge, a shot Allen describes as his "attempt to set the romantic vision of New York against the mess that people make of their lives" (113–114), the spiritual malaise of the two figures within the shot lend to it a quality of despair recalling Eliots' bridge, where "Under the brown fog of a winter dawn, / A crowd flooded over," a bridge where "Sighs, short and infrequent, were exhaled, / And each man fixed his eyes before his feet" (61, 64–65). The affair thus begun before the bridge is, because of each character's insurmountable neuroses, doomed from the outset, and the contaminated water that flows beneath this bridge of sighs makes its way even into the lovers' room. One need only look to the brown water in Ike's apartment to recognize in it a potential symbol of contamination of the channels of sexual and verbal communication. It is significant that the woman who shares a glass of it with him is the equally miserable and emotionally confused Mary. Theirs is a union of faked orgasms and frustrated conversations. When Ike and Mary argue, she expresses frustration with his refusal to get angry and "get things out into the open." He responds by telling her he does not react that way, but rather internalizes things: "I don't get angry, I grow a tumor instead."

The spiritual decay thus far considered has physical, if imagined, correlatives in the host of diseases that plague Allen's various protagonists. Ike is certain that nearly everything causes cancer based on what he calls "gut feeling." In Allen's *Annie Hall* (1977), Alvy fears skin cancer from playing tennis in the sun. Later, in *Hannah and Her Sisters* (1986), Mickey believes he has the classic symptoms of inoperable brain cancer. Such well documented hypochondriasis in Allen's films, such compulsion to invent fatal maladies for oneself, suggests a physical dodge of a spiritual illness that none of the protagonists are able to articulate in spiritual terms. They do try, though; many of Allen's troubled urbanites have analysts. However, few of these analysts, if any, succeed in helping Allen's neurotic protagonists. Clearly Allen has little faith in the disciples of Freud and Jung to effect any psychic ease in these men and women.

Yet even the armchair analyst would remark on the fact that the Allen king's overmastering sexual drive never yields him happiness or

moral compass, leading more often than not to confusion and misery.
The archetypal scenario for so many incarnations of the Woody Allen
urban neurotic, and one that his relationships with precocious nymphets
in films such as his *Husbands and Wives*, (1992), and *Manhattan* attempt
to resolve, is that of the king of New York City in spiritual decline. His
only hope lies in a spiritual rejuvenation he obsessively quests for
through the expediency of repeated, and often misguided, sexual encounters. Sexual potency, an obsession of Allen protagonists in nearly all his
films, is a constant reaffirmation of vitality. The recurrent assertion of
what Ike describes as his "astonishing sexual technique" evinces a
"protests too much" response in the audience familiar with his body of
work. The more disquieting manifestations of this obsession, such as his
advice to his prepubescent son in *Manhattan*, about picking up women in
the Russian Tearoom, only emphasize the near mania of Allen protagonists to assert their virility. The sexual effort, however excessive, is motivated by a desire for a type of rejuvenation or replenishment of the moral
landscape.

As early as 1922, James Frazer accounted for sexual excesses, albeit
toward the rejuvenation not of soul but of soil, in *The Golden Bough*:
"We might assume with a high degree of probability that the profligacy
which notoriously attended these [vegetation] ceremonies was at one
time not an accidental excess but an essential part of the rites" (257).
While Frazer went on to admit that at the time of his writing it "might
perhaps be vain to look in civilised Europe for customs of this sort," he
allows that the "ruder races in other parts of the world have consciously
employed the intercourse of the sexes as a means to insure the fruitfulness of the earth" (257). It appears the "ruder races" of Allen's Manhattan have employed sex, unsuccessfully, to redeem a spiritual wasteland.
Jill describes sex with Ike as an empty experience, a "sham." And Ike
cannot help but suspect that Mary, who lives almost entirely in the mind,
has faked her orgasm with him. Similarly, the union of his best friend
Yale and his wife Emily breeds neither children nor contentment; Emily
pines for the family Yale refuses to give her, and Yale pursues a doomed
affair with Mary. The sterility of sexual union in so many of Allen's films
resists even the prodigality of what might be called the protagonists'
"will to shutup." Those unions that do produce children (they almost
never yield contentment), such as that of Jill and Ike in *Manhattan*, fail,
and the child's interests become those of the mother or, what Ike finds
even more disturbing, those of the lesbian lover who has usurped his
throne. Tracy, then, would serve Weston's analysis of the Fisher King

scenario as the quester whose mission is "to break the spell which retains the Grail King *in a semblance of life*, and we learn, by implication, that the land is restored to fruitfulness" (12, italics mine). Life for Ike is only a semblance because one gets the sense that he has always one thought in death or misery. Ike is not altogether different from Alvy Singer, who in *Annie Hall* neatly divided life between the miserable and the horrible. Jill, while her account is certainly biased, suspects this as well, and writes as much in the tell-all book Ike discovers in a bookseller's window while on holiday with Yale and friends. Naturally curious, and amused by Isaac's discomfort, Yale reads aloud Jill's assessment:

> He was given to fits of rage, Jewish liberal paranoia, male chau-
> vinism, self-righteous misanthropy, and nihilistic moods of de-
> spair. He had complaints about life but never any solutions. He
> longed to be an artist, but balked at the necessary sacrifices. In
> his most private moments he spoke of his fear of death, which
> he elevated to tragic heights, when in fact it was mere narcis-
> sism.

This is perhaps an even more powerful indictment of Ike's existen-tial impotence than her preference for another woman. For all Ike's protests of Jill's malice and the injustice of her claims, even the casual observer of Woody Allen's oeuvre will recognize in this summary the dark side of the Woody Allen persona. Perhaps labeling it the dark side is not really accurate either, for it is ever present, buoyed, masked or de-fused by skillfully-crafted and well-timed one liners or preemptive self-deprecation. But it is there all the same.

Woody Allen and, by extension, his filmic surrogate, is the exemplar of the popular conception of New York City as the Mecca of liberality, intellectualism, and (resultant) neuroses. "New York," claims Ike, "was his town, and always would be," but the often paralyzing neuroses of Ike and the other inhabitants of *Manhattan* recall Weston's observation that, like the Fisher King and the Waste, the emotional sterility of one effects that of the other: "the misfortune which has fallen upon the country is that of a prolonged drought, which has destroyed vegetation, and left the land Waste; the effect of the hero's question is to restore the water to their channel, and render the land once more fertile" (19).

To achieve this, Allen must go beyond conventional morality, mov-ing toward a younger woman and an earlier faith in the redemptive power of purity. Admittedly, Allen has provided his redeemer with little competition. Ike's love affairs are amusing disasters, and their air of impossibility seems deliberately engineered by Allen to set off the simplicity and contentment Ike enjoys with Tracy. His first wife becomes a Moony, gets into ESP, then segues hilariously into the corporate amorality of the William Morris Agency. The second wife, Jill, is but a temporary convert to heterosexuality, and divorces Ike for another woman. And Mary is a lovely but insufferable bundle of narcissism and neuroses. A revealing juxtaposition of scenes makes it plain that only with Tracy is Ike truly alive.

Ike's baffled attitude while exiting the Colony theater, where the tragically cerebral Mary has dragged him for a screening of Dovzhenko's *Earth,* stands in suggestive contrast to the warm and genuine repose of an earlier tableau of Ike sitting in bed with Tracy, eating Chinese food and watching a W.C. Fields movie. Clearly he is happier with the innocent, though in characteristic Allen fashion, Ike cannot allow himself to enjoy this. However he undermines his own happiness, his preference for Tracy derives poignancy less from the surface incongruity of a mature man's desire for a girl-woman, than from the spiritual desolation this need for youthful vitality hints at, the fundamental pathos of the Allen urbanite. Tracy's quest, in short, is to restore spiritual vitality, a renewed faith in humanity, to the spiritually enervated fisher king, who will then project a rejuvenated spiritual landscape from his own mind. The success of this quest is put into doubt, however, by Ike's equivocal smile, the last shot of the film. Tracy has assured him that "not every one gets corrupted," and tells him and that he has to "have a little faith in people." Richard A. Blake, in *Woody Allen: Profane and Sacred*, sees Ike's smile as "magnificently ambiguous," and poses ultimately unanswerable questions as to its significance:

> Has Ike (Allen himself) finally understood that it is possible for human integrity and moral living to exist in the chaotic universe he has imagined in to Manhattan? And does that thought make him happy? Or does he smile because Tracy has the wisdom to leave this jumbled universe with its twisted relationships to try to make some sense out of her world through art in London? Or finally is the smile a kind of cynical comment on her youthful naivete? (80).

Again, it is impossible to say. In a modern urban context, Grail myths can only end in equivocal grins. A possible solution to the spiritual malaise of modern urban life has been proffered nonetheless, and Ike's probable rejection of Tracy's revitalizing influence speaks less of her ultimate failure to save him than his perverse refusal to be saved.

In *Annie Hall*, Alvy Singer undertook the tutelage of a naïve and seemingly aimless woman. Charmed by her "la dee da" befuddlement, he eagerly embarked on her tutelage in the politics of the miserable and the horrible, with Max Ophul's *The Sorrow and The Pity* as one of his preferred texts. By *Manhattan*, Allen, through Ike, has moved beyond a childlike woman to an actual child. There are concessions to the sentinels of conventional morality; Tracy often demonstrates a wisdom and perspective that surpass Ike's, and he twice tells her not to be so mature about things. He also protests the impossibility of the relationship to Tracy, Yale and Yale's wife Emily. He even breaks up with her. But Allen clearly means us to recognize that only with Tracy is Ike truly comfortable. Ultimately, it seems necessary to mitigate the age discrepancy only if we are to understand the characters as realistic. And, Blake reminds us, this is a tempting but misleading interpretation:

> To reduce the characters to realism is to misconstrue Allen's point. Tracy represents beauty, purity and hope in Ike's tortured world. . . . Contact with love in its purest form, with an "innocent" girl who teaches him how to enter love as a giving relationship, holds a profoundly moral meaning for Allen and his audience, this growth through altruism provides a theological model for the human relationship with others and ultimately for the human person's relationship with God. (84)

Whether the audience derives a "profoundly moral" meaning from Ike's relationship with a 17-year old depends on their ability briefly to relinquish for a time the tendency to regard the film as realistic and thus to discard the strictures of bourgeois morality. They must instead recognize the story as a wistful quest for redemption. After all, that Ike replies to Yale's accusation, "You think you're God!" with "I've gotta model myself on *someone*!" semi-seriously points to Ike's desire to attain a certain moral order to his universe. His choice of Tracy as the means to this end suggests, however, a need to transcend contemporary social mores. He sacrifices conventional morality for archetype, unconsciously invoking an old legend of purity rejuvenating a spiritually withered landscape.

Toward film's end, Ike speaks into a tape recorder an idea he has for a short story "about people in Manhattan who are constantly creating these real unnecessary neurotic problems for themselves, cause it keeps them from dealing with more unsolvable, terrifying problems about the universe." The inhabitants of Allen's island of *Manhattan*, and indeed of much of his opus, create obsessions, fixations, and intellectual preoccupations in order to distract themselves from the fundamental alienation of modern existence. That these foibles are more often than not rendered with wit and empathy only makes more palatable their familiarity to the audience. Or perhaps it distracts them from the potential application of Allen's fables to their own lives. And ultimately *Manhattan* is a fable, about a older man who identifies himself with a city of surface vibrancy but spiritual decline, and who sees as his only hope for rejuvenation a young woman refreshingly free of pretense and neurosis who, if he will let her, will restore his faith in humanity.

Works Cited

Allen, Woody and Marshall Brickman. *Manhattan*. Rollins-Joffe/United Artists, 1979.

Blake, Richard A. *Woody Allen: Profane and Sacred*. London: The Scarecrow Press, 1995.

Eliot, T.S. *The Waste Land*. The Norton Anthology of American Literature, 3rd ed. New York: W.W. Norton & Co., 1989.

Frazer, Sir James George. *The Golden Bough*. New York: Touchstone, 1996.

Weston, Jessie. *From Ritual to Romance*. Mineola: Dover Publications, Inc., 1997.

Existential Themes in Woody Allen's *Crimes and Misdemeanors* with Reference to *Annie Hall* and *Hannah and Her Sisters*

SANDER H. LEE

Philosophers argue about everything. For example, philosophers love to debate about labels like "existentialism." Existentialism is a name given to a philosophical movement which became popular in the decades following World War II. The philosopher most associated with this movement was the Frenchman, Jean-Paul Sartre. While Sartre may not have coined the term, he was well-known for his willingness to describe himself as an existentialist.

In fact, in France and much of Europe, Sartre became as recognizable a figure as a movie star or a sports hero. In the United States, the image of the gloomy existentialist dressed all in black with his beard or goatee drinking wine in a smoke-filled jazz club became a cliche on TV and in films. This image also became associated in people's mind with that of the '50s "beatnik."

For a classic example of this popular stereotype, take a look at the 1957 film *Funny Face* in which a sophisticated Fred Astaire transforms Audry Hepburn from an unhappy beat existentialist into a glamorous fashion model. This story was a variation on a theme found in an earlier film, the wonderful 1939 *Ninotchka,* in which a sophisticated Melvyn Douglas transforms Greta Garbo from a dour Communist functionary into a glamorous woman of the world. Indeed, for many, the popular images of the existentialist and the revolutionary Marxist blur together, partially because Sartre himself attempted to combine the two.

But Sartre's atheistic approach is not the only philosophy which has been labelled as "existentialism." In the wake of its postwar popularity, a number of commentators, such as Walter Kaufmann and William Barrett, made the argument that existentialism was a set of themes or concerns, and that, perhaps, a number of philosophers who wrote before Sartre, and had never even heard the word "existentialism," could accurately be described as important influences on its development. Two of the philosophers often named in this connection are the nineteenth century theorists Soren Kierkegaard and Frederick Nietzsche.

In addition, in their books on existentialism, these same commentators also included twentieth century philosophers who may have heard of existentialism but either did not actively associate themselves with the movement or actually denied that their philosophy should be identified with it at all. For example, both Martin Heidegger and Albert Camus were very well aware of Sartre's philosophy and publicly disassociated themselves from it. Yet, in Kaufmann and Barrett's books on existentialism, and in many of those which followed, both Heidegger and Camus are discussed extensively in the context of existentialism, even though Kaufmann, for one, is careful to acknowledge that neither philosopher considered himself to actually be an "existentialist."

Further, there are those philosophers of the twentieth century who were willing, or even eager, to accept the label of "existentialist" despite the fact that their philosophies would appear, on the face of them, to differ significantly from Sartre on important issues such as religious faith. In this group could be placed such contemporary religious philosophers as Martin Buber, Gabriel Marcel, Paul Tillich, and Joseph B. Soloveitchik.

So, given all this, what does it mean to say that someone is an existentialist? According to Walter Kaufmann, "The refusal to belong to any school of thought, the repudiation of the adequacy of any body of beliefs whatever, and especially of systems, and a marked dissatisfaction with traditional philosophy as superficial, academic, and remote from life—that is the heart of existentialism" (12). He also says that, "The existentialist has taken up the passionate concern with questions that arise from life, the moral pathos, and the firm belief that, to be serious, a philosophy has to be lived" (51).

So, from this, existentialism sounds like no more than an attitude, a rebellious and passionate commitment to living, but one with no particular beliefs. Yet it must be more than just that or all rebellious and passionate people would be existentialists, a group which could arguably include both Socrates and Adolf Hitler! However, no one who knows anything about the movement would seriously consider either of those two to be members. So we need to know more about what makes someone an existentialist.

In his 1996 book *Existentialist Philosophy: An Introduction*, L. Nathan Oaklander points out that:

> Books on existentialism often stress certain themes that are shared by a variety of philosophers who are called "existentialists." One common theme is the emphasis on human freedom and the related Sartrean slogan that "existence precedes essence," meaning that we have no prepackaged essence or nature, but that what we are is what we choose to be. Another theme stressed by existentialists is the contingency of the world, the fact that the universe has no meaning and is absurd. A third is that there are no objective values. (7)

This helps, but it still doesn't make entirely clear what most existentialists agree on and what they are most likely to disagree about among themselves. I believe that one of the best sources for clarifying these two issues is the Woody Allen film *Crimes and Misdemeanors* made in 1989.

* * *

In this essay, I will explore some of the fundamental issues and debates within existentialism by using elements from this film as examples. My discussion will assume that you have seen the film recently and remember both the plot and the names of the characters (see filmography of the end of this essay to refresh your memory).

In the voiceover narration which plays over a montage of scenes at the end of *Crimes and Misdemeanors*, Allen gives us one of the best short descriptions of existential beliefs I have ever heard or read. This narration is spoken by Professor Louis Levy (Martin Bergmann), the Holocaust survivor who commits suicide in the course of the film:

> We are all faced throughout our lives with agonizing decisions, moral choices. Some are on a grand scale, most of these choices are on lesser points, but, we define ourselves by the choices we have made. We are, in fact, the sum total of our choices. We wince and fall so unpredictably, so unfairly, human happiness does not seem to have been included in the design of creation.

Here, Allen has Levy state many of the same claims as Oaklander, but in a manner which better conveys the passion of which we spoke earlier. In my view, all existentialists worthy of the label would agree with Levy in the above quote. Allen then has Levy end the narration with an expression of what I would call the more optimistic, possibly even religious form of existentialism:

> It is only we, with our capacity to love, that give meaning to the indifferent universe. And yet, most human beings seem to have the ability to keep trying, and even to find joy, from simple things like the family, their work, and from the hope that future generations might understand more.

At these last lines, Allen returns us to the scene of the blind rabbi Ben (Sam Waterston) dancing sweetly with his daughter at her wedding. As Levy's voice fades out, so does the quiet music accompanying it. Ben and his daughter stop dancing and she kisses his cheek as the crowd applauds approvingly. She is clearly the symbol of the future generation to which Levy refers, and her adoration for her saintly father, and the approval of the crowd, suggest that there are real reasons for hope.

The first part of Levy's soliloquy contains all the elements of a Sartrean existential analysis of the possibilities for authentic moral projects in an indifferent universe in which all meaning springs from the ways in which we exercise our freedom and take responsibility for our acts. We can no longer expect an all-powerful God to intervene into human affairs to right our wrongs or cure the evils of society. If we wish to live authentically in accordance with moral principles which we construct for ourselves, then we each must take the responsibility for creating the meaning for our own lives, and committing ourselves to act in accordance with those principles, even when this means making material sacrifice.

Before going further with the analysis of existential themes in *Crimes and Misdemeanors*, I must stop to answer an obvious question: why should we take Woody Allen seriously? To many, Allen is unquestionably better known for his highly publicized personal problems and for his early work as a comedian than for the serious exploration of philosophical themes which characterize his later films, films such as *Crimes and Misdemeanors*. While Allen is generally conceded to be a master of the comic genre in which he begun, one worthy of serious study whose work has greatly influenced others, many look with disfavor towards his efforts at creating more serious films.

Allen has developed into one of our most important American film artists. From a philosophical standpoint, his films are of enormous import in that they are obsessed with issues of contemporary metaphysical concern. Philosophically, perhaps the greatest tension within Allen's work is between the desire of many of his characters to ground their lives in a set of traditional ethical values while, simultaneously, they sadly acknowledge that no foundation can currently be found to justify such a belief. This tension could indeed be called "the existential dilemma," as it plays a vital role in the work of a variety of "existential" philosophers such as Kierkegaard, Buber, and Sartre.

Within his films there exists an ongoing conflict between despair and a hope based on some sort of faith, a love/hate relationship with God in which Allen's intellectual tendency towards Sartrean atheism combats his spiritual yearning for some form of salvation. As one way of portraying Allen's inner religious struggles, I will use some of the ideas presented by Rabbi Joseph B. Soloveitchik in his lengthy essay, "The Lonely Man of Faith," which was written in March 1965 as a statement of Jewish existentialism for the journal *Tradition*, but which has been recently republished in book form for the first time.

Throughout Allen's career, he has frequently been accused of narcissism and the advocacy of moral relativism, when in fact he has been, and continues to be, one of film's most forceful advocates of the importance that an awareness of moral values plays in any meaningful life. Indeed, the one theme which permeates all of his films derives from his contention that contemporary American society is rapidly descending into barbarism precisely because of our societal failure to maintain our sense of individual moral responsibility.

In his films, as in his earlier comedic work, Allen demonstrates an awareness and understanding of the history of Western Philosophy which is quite extraordinary for a man whose formal education ended at the age of nineteen when he was ejected from New York University. His early parodies of traditional philosophical concerns (such as in his essays "My Philosophy" and "Mr. Big" from the 1971 book of essays *Getting Even*) show that even then, Allen had read and thought about serious philosophical issues. In the first five films he directed, ending with Love and Death, Allen continued to comedically explore traditional philosophical concerns, including, in the last film, parodies of Tolstoy's musings in *War and Peace* as well as Ingmar Bergman's obsessions with human mortality in *The Seventh Seal*.

Starting with *Annie Hall* (1977), Allen's first really serious film, elements of his own philosophical concerns appear in ways that are no longer primarily comedic. Structured in the form of a long therapy session, this film begins and ends with Allen's persona, Alvy Singer, telling us jokes which are more serious than funny. It is in this film that Allen perfects his technique of using humor to genuinely explore philosophical issues, as opposed to his earlier practice of doing just the opposite, that is, exploiting traditional philosophical concerns in order to be humorous.

Allen's distinctive wit is the thread which runs throughout all of the characters he has played. Allen's humor imposes a running commentary on all the events in his films, a commentary which proclaims his unique identity and his existential rebellion against the traditional behavior of others. Whether he is tearing up his driver's license as he explains to a policeman that he has always had a problem with authority, as he does in *Annie Hall*, or portraying his employer, a successful television producer, as a clone of Mussolini, as he does later in *Crimes and Misdemeanors*; Allen's humor always distances him from others by proclaiming his rebellious passion, the same passion described by Kaufmann.

Yet, in Allen's films, there is never a claim that humor can fulfill his characters' goals or even uncover the truth. Alvy Singer can only get Annie to return to New York in his fictional play, not in the reality of the film. Alvy's obsession with his own mortality, his condemnation of the lax moral values of Los Angeles, and his attempt to create meaning for his life through his destructive relationship with Annie, are all vital elements of the philosophical themes which will haunt Allen's work throughout the rest of his career.

Allen's existentialism is portrayed most powerfully in *Crimes and Misdemeanors*, his best film to date, in which the main character, Judah Rosenthal (Martin Landau), comes to "see" that in a world devoid of a divine presence, all acts are permissible, even murder. The apparent philosophical despair of this film, in which the most moral individual, a rabbi, is shown gradually going blind, has been taken by many to symbolize Allen's ultimate sense of hopelessness.

In this film, all of the supposedly "virtuous" characters are shown wearing glasses because of their inability to see the true nature of the world. As the film progresses, one character, Halley (Mia Farrow), is apparently able to discard her glasses only once she has also discarded her values by agreeing to marry the arrogant, pompous but successful TV producer Lester (Alan Alda). Allen's character, Cliff Stern, is punished for his commitment to his beliefs as we see him lose everything he cared for; his love, his work, and even his spiritual mentor, the philosophy professor Louis Levy (Martin Bergmann), who, like Primo Levi, survived the Holocaustbut responds to the petty immoralities of everyday life by killing himself.

Most ominously, Judah, who bears the name of one of the greatest fighters for traditional Jewish values and heritage, Judah Maccabee betrays the faith of his father Sol (David Howard) by not only committing a murder; but also renouncing the consequences of his guilt in a universe which he declares to be indifferent to our actions. These themes are introduced from the very beginning of the film when we hear Judah address the audience at a banquet given in his honor. Commenting on completion of the hospital's new opthamology wing he comments on a remark made by his father when he was a child: "I remember my father telling me, 'the eyes of God are on us always!' The eyes of God! What a phrase to a young boy! And what were God's eyes like? Unimaginatively penetrating and intense eyes I assumed. And I wonder if it was just a coincidence that I made my specialty ophthalmology?" At the words "even as a child," we are shown two Orthodox Jewish men sitting in the front of a synagogue reading sacred texts as they each sway back and forth in the traditional fashion.

In these first scenes, Allen establishes the conflicting elements which will dominate his starkest investigation yet into the increasing moral and religious paralysis which grips contemporary American society. By giving his protagonist the first name of "Judah," and so explicitly showing us his Orthodox Jewish upbringing, Allen makes clear his intention to explore the role of religion, specifically the role of Judaism, in the story he is about to tell. Although we see in his speech at the testimonial dinner that he still carries with him a sense of obligation towards his Jewish heritage and the values it epitomizes, Judah can not bring himself to resist the temptation to follow his reason alone and deny the objective existence of all values.

The conflict between reason and faith is presented explicitly in many of the film's relationships. For Judah sees primarily the emptiness and harshness of the world while his brother, Ben, believes in a universe with moral structure, guided by a higher power.

Thus, the differing philosophies of two brothers, the fundamental conflict which resides in all of Allen's films is laid bare for our inspection. This conflict, which I have called "the existential dilemma," pits our recognition of the claim that there can be no rational basis for grounding values, against our need to conduct our lives in accordance with a set of just such standards. Here we see the conflict between the hedonism of what Joseph Soloveitchik calls "Adam the first" (represented here by Judah) and the redemptive spirit of what he calls "Adam the second"(Ben).

Soloveitchik, an Orthodox rabbi who wished to reconcile the demands of faith with life in contemporary secular society, writes of these two fundamentally opposed images of humanity which can be found in the Orthodox Halakhic Scriptures.

Adam the first, whom he also calls "majestic man," is motivated by his natural desire to fulfill his freedom through the creation of dignity in a human community. This he achieves through behavior which strives to control his environment using the tools of his mind and his creativity. Adam the first believes that one can come to learn everything, to penetrate the secrets of the universe if only one persistently accumulates enough data, enough facts. Yet, Adam the first, a Sartrean existentialist, is also aware of his freedom and the responsibility which flows from that freedom to create meaning for the world both in work and in one's relations with others. Adam the first is a social contract theorist who constructs a stable social environment through the creation of laws and institutions to enforce those laws.

Soloveitchik states:

> Adam the first is not only a creative theoretician. He is also a creative aesthetic. He fashions ideas with his mind, and beauty with his heart. He enjoys both his intellectual and his aesthetic creativity and takes pride in it. He also displays creativity in the world of the norm: he legislates for himself norms and laws because a dignified existence is an orderly one.
>
> Anarchy and dignity are mutually exclusive. He is this-worldly-minded, finitude-oriented, beauty-centered. Adam the first is always an aesthete, whether engaged in an intellectual or in an ethical performance. His conscience is energized not by the idea of the idea of the good, but by that of the beautiful. His mind is questing not for the true, but for the pleasant and functional, which are rooted in the aesthetical, not the noetic-ethical sphere. (18–19).

For Soloveitchik, Adam the second:

> sees his separateness from nature and his existential uniqueness not in dignity or majesty but in something else. There is, in his opinion, another mode of existence through which a man can find his own self, namely, the redemptive, which is not necessarily identical with the dignified. (25)

Unlike Adam the first, Adam the second experiences himself as incomplete and fundamentally alone. For Soloveitchik, "loneliness is nothing but the act of questioning one's own ontological legitimacy, worth, and reasonableness." (31)

According to Soloveitchik:

> Adam the second suddenly finds out that he is alone, that he has alienated himself from the world of the brute and instinctual mechanical state of an outward existence, while he has failed to ally himself with the intelligent, purposive inward beings who inhabit the new world into which he has entered. Every great redemptive step forward entails the ever-growing tragic awareness of his aloneness and only-ness and consequently of his loneliness and insecurity. . . . At this crucial point, if Adam is to bring his quest for redemption to full realization, he must initiate action leading to the discovery of a companion who, even though as unique and singular as he, will master the art of communicating and, with him, form a community. However, this action, since it is part of the redemptive gesture, must also be sacrificial. The medium of attaining full redemption is defeat. This new companionship is not attained through conquest, but through surrender and retreat. . . Thus, in crisis and distress there was planted the seed of a new type of community—the faith community which reached full fruition in the covenant between God and Abraham. (37– 39)

This new covenant results from a Kierkegaardian leap of faith in the redemptive power of love. For Soloveitchik, the relationship between Adam the first and second is a dialectical one which requires an ongoing interplay between the two. Soloveitchik states that:

> since the dialectical role has been assigned to man by God, it is God who wants the man of faith to oscillate between the faith community and the community of majesty, between being confronted by God in the cosmos and the intimate, immediate apprehension of God through the covenant, and who therefore willed that complete human redemption be unattainable. (86)

While Ben and Judah are in one sense represented as the two extremes on these issues, in another sense, as Ben has just told us, this conflict is really taking place within Judah. Judah does have a spark of Ben's faith within him and the film's primary drama turns on his decision as to how to resolve this crisis and the consequences of that decision. When Ben says that they have moved "from a small infidelity to the meaning of existence," he suggests an interpretation of both the film's title and the inter-relationship between its two plotlines. How one acts to deal with "a small infidelity" determines one's position on the very "meaning of existence." The distance between such small misdemeanors and unforgivable crimes is much shorter than normally thought, once one has rejected all notions of values and responsibility.

This point is very similar to the one made in the novel whose title most resembles that of this film, namely Dostoyevsky's *Crime and Punishment*. In that book, an author who (like Kierkegaard or Soloveitchik) has made the "leap to faith" while acknowledging the apparent fundamental absurdity of the world, shows us how the failure to make that leap leads a student named Raskolnikov, overcome by existential dread, to murder an elderly woman. Through his dialogue with his pursuer, and his own corresponding internal debate, Raskolnikov is led by the novel's end to a genuine acceptance of the possibility of religious redemption.

Interestingly, Judah's situation requires that, in order to accept Ben's challenge, he must choose to have faith not directly in God, but (like Buber) in the redemptive power of a renewal of an authentic "I-Thou" relationship with his wife Miriam (Claire Bloom). Judah must decide if he can trust Miriam sufficiently to chance the possibility that the revelation of his sin will destroy both of their lives. If he decides that he does not trust her enough to take this risk, then one must wonder at his reasons for wishing to maintain his marriage with her.

At a surprise birthday celebration at home with his family, Judah is given a treadmill. Confirming the hint that his family represents a form of staid boredom while his mistress Dolores (Anjelica Huston) brings with her excitement and melodrama, Judah is called to the phone to hear Dolores' threat to be at his house in five minutes if he doesn't meet her at the gas station down the road. Ominous sounds of thunder accompany her threats and by the time Judah arrives to meet her, a full-fledged storm is in progress.

Sitting in a car, Dolores demands that they go away together and that, when they return, Judah must "bring things with Miriam to an conclusion." She also gives him a birthday present, an album of Schubert's music. Her choice of birthday present, a gift of the music she knows he loves, suggests that she represents the desires of his soul while Miriam's treadmill is the symbol the dullness of his respectable married life.

The sound of thunder accompanied by a brilliant flash of lightening announce Judah's appearance as he descends the stairs back at home with Ben's words about morality and forgiveness racing through his mind. Images of hellfire surround him as he stares in the burning fireplace and ignites a cigarette with his lighter. Sitting on a sofa, Ben's voice manifests itself into a fantasy of his actual presence as he tries to persuade Judah to give up the murderous schemes of his brother Jack (Jerry Orbach) in order to ask the world, and God, for forgiveness. Judah rejects Ben's arguments, and when Ben mentions God, Judah reveals that Jack has at last convinced him to become a hedonistic nihilist, Judah picks up the phone, calls Jack, and tells him "to move ahead with what we discussed. How much will you need?" Judah has now resolved to place his own selfish interests over the law, morality, and God and to order the killing of Dolores. In doing so, he explicitly abandons the faith of his fathers and places himself outside of God's realm. His self-deception is massive in his refusal to take any responsibility for creating his predicament (he claims that the real world "found him" as though he did nothing to bring it about), and in his refusal to consider the possibility that he may truly deserve what is happening to him.

Judah's namesake, the Maccabee, gave up his life to fight for his father's faith against the superior military forces of his people's oppressors. The original Judah did nothing to "deserve" his fate, yet he never questioned his obligation to sacrifice everything in this cause. The contemporary Judah expects to be handed a life of wealth and comfort without sacrifice. Like Dr. Faustus, Judah is willing to sell his soul to Mephistopheles in exchange for the satisfaction of his desires. In his fantasized dialogue with Ben, he is so mired in lies that he won't even allow Ben to use his strongest argument (that Judah is cold-bloodedly plotting a murder), restricting him to references of "sweeping her under the rug" instead. As a result of this betrayal of his heritage and the best part of himself, we expect to see him punished both by society, and, if we believe, by God.

After the murder has taken place, and Judah has visited the scene to remove incriminating documents, we see him back at home, sitting alone in the bathroom with the lights on while an unaware Miriam sleeps soundly in the bedroom. Suddenly, the phone begins to ring. Judah rushes to answer it only to find there is no one on the other end of the line, suggesting that God is calling Judah to task for his crime, yet refusing to speak to him directly.

Later, overwhelmed by a sense of guilt, he goes to the home of his youth and asks the current owner if he may look around. He tells her of his memories of playing with Jack there and of the high expectations they all had of him, expectations that were never fulfilled. Suddenly, he hears the sound of a Passover seder emanating from the dining room. Standing in the doorway, he watches as his imagination creates a seder from his youth.

The first sounds he hears are those of the Hebrew prayers over the eating of the bitter herbs. The seder is a dinner service performed at home with the head of the family, in this case Judah's father Sol (David Howard), leading the service and explaining its meaning as he sits at the table's head. The eating of the bitter herbs represents the suffering of the Jews when they were slaves in Egypt until Moses came, with God's help, to lead his people into freedom in the promised land.

We listen as Judah's Aunt May (Anna Berger) challenges Sol by questioning the legitimacy of the "mumbo-jumbo" of the religious service. Calling her a "Leninist," Sol acts offended by the tone of her comments as she questions the existence of any objective set of moral values and argues that "might makes right" even when it comes to the Holocaust.

This scene contains the most complete discussion of morality and faith to be found in any of Allen's films. In fact, it is so powerful that it could stand alone as a superb discussion of philosophical issues, comparable to the famous "Legend of the Grand Inquisitor" section from Dostoyevsky's *The Brothers Karamazov*. Like that passage, this scene contains a dialogue between those who favor a nihilist view of the universe as a meaningless, mechanical environment in which we are completely free to create the meaning of our lives however we wish; and the believer who uses the same freedom to choose to have faith in God and morality despite the fact that he may be willing to acknowledge that there is no rational basis for that faith. Thus, in this debate, we revisit the distinction made by Soloveitchik in his discussion of the conflict between Adam the first and Adam the second.

The "nihilists" (Aunt May and her supporters) take a position resembling not only that of the Grand Inquisitor, but also that of a variety of philosophers from throughout Western history including the Sartrean existentialist. Like Soloveitchik's "majestic man," they favor the evidence of the senses and the scientific use of reason over the desires and beliefs of the "soul." The "believer" (Sol), on the other hand, takes a position resembling the more mystical religious traditions which culminate in the existential theories of theists such as Kierkegaard, Marcel, Buber, and Soloveitchik.

The dialogue also reminds us of Socrates' debate with the Sophist Thrasymachus in one section of Plato's best known dialogue, *The Republic*. Like Thrasymachus, May argues that what is just is "whatever is in the interest of the stronger party." For Thrasymachus, what was important was to appear to the world at large as a just, honorable person while, simultaneously, acting unjustly so as to get away with as much as possible. While Socrates is able to defeat the Sophist's arguments in the context of this dialogue, Plato's opponents have always contended that this was made possible only because Plato purposely did not allow Thrasymachus to give the best possible arguments.

Allen does not similarly handcuff the nihilists in this scene. Their arguments are presented so compellingly that it is made clear that this incident from his youth contributed greatly to Judah's later choice of the rational life of the man of science over that of the believer which his father wanted so much for him. May's use of the fact of the Holocaust adds to the potency of her position and is worth a more detailed examination. For the sake of this discussion, I will temporarily play devil's advocate by expanding her arguments.

For May, one of the most striking moral implications of the Holocaust lies in the fact that it vividly demonstrates that human beings can violently disagree concerning the moral principles which they adopt. The fundamental assumption underlying natural law theory (the position for which the Man in the Hat appears to argue) states that, while people of good intent might legitimately disagree over many normative issues, ultimately there exists a universal set of underlying basic principles to which we all can and should agree.

But, May would counter, in the twentieth century, if we have learned anything, it is that people do not agree on many fundamental principles of value. Debates and disagreements over such issues have characterized numerous international communications. Thus, perhaps the most difficult problem facing natural law theorists is not just that of deciding what these natural laws are, but also that of persuading others to adopt them or of forcibly imposing them upon people who disagree, which would only result in the confirmation of May's contention that "might makes right."

Thus, May contends, the role of morality in each individual's life is only what they choose it to be. If one wishes to uphold "morality," however one defines it, then one may do so. If, on the other hand, one wishes to ignore the issues of morality altogether, and commit a crime, even murder, then there is nothing to stop you other than your own conscience ("And I say, if he can do it, and get away with it, and he chooses not to be bothered by the ethics, then he's home free.") There is no question that the arguments of the nihilist in this scene overwhelm the naturalist claims of the Man in the Hat that we are all basically "decent," and, it is implied, all agree on the most important fundamental values.

Even more compelling for the nihilists' position is the question as to how God could have allowed the Holocaust to take place. How could an all-powerful, caring God have stood by and allowed millions of innocent people to die without intervening as He is claimed to have done during the story of the original Passover, the Exodus from Egypt?

Yet, Allen's presentation of Sol's position is also compelling in its own way. While acknowledging that his position is based on faith rather than logic and reason, Sol ultimately claims that the life of the man of faith, Soloveitchik's Adam the second, is more fulfilling than that of the nihilists' Adam the first. As we discussed earlier, Adam the second makes the giant Kierkegaardian leap of faith into belief without the safety net of logic or evidence. Given the fact that he feels that a life without morality or God is a meaningless one which can only end in bitterness and despair, he chooses to believe, precisely because there is no reason to do so, in a sacrificial act analogous to that of Abraham in choosing to obey God's command to sacrifice Isaac despite the dictates of both his desires and his reason.

Even if there is no God, if one's faith is a denial of the "truth," it is better to believe than not to believe because only through belief can the spiritual lifestyle, the only one capable of fulfilling our deepest human needs, be attained. For Sol, the existential human condition is such that each of us *must* choose the values by which we will live. Even those, like the nihilist, who claim to have chosen to deny all values are making a choice which implies its own set of values. The nihilisys' choice ultimately implies the acceptance of the ethic of hedonism, the belief that one is justified in doing whatever one wishes. This is itself a value system which posits the worth of individual pleasure over the demands of a traditional morality and religion.

It is impossible to avoid responsibility for choosing some values, every act in which one engages represents a favoring of the worth of that action over all the others available to one at that moment. Therefore, since one must choose to believe in something, and that choice must be made without any objective knowledge of right and wrong, one should choose those values which best correspond to one's vision of how the universe *ought to be*. For Sol, this means that one should choose to believe in a universe governed by a caring and moral God who may not directly intervene in human affairs, or manifest His presence in any concrete fashion. One should choose to do this not because one can know with certainty that such a God exists, but, instead, because without such a belief life would not be worth living.

In this sense, the woman at the seder table is right in comparing Sol's choice to have faith to the aesthetic activity of an artist, but wrong in suggesting that only those born with "a gift" have the capacity to do this. For, according to the existentialists, such as Sartre, the human condition is such that *all of us* are condemned to create the meaning of our lives on the basis of our freedom. Thus, Sol is not unusual in his *ability* to have faith, but only in *the strength of his commitment* to that faith. Sartre makes a similar point about the relationship between art and morality in his essay, "Existentialism is a Humanism":

> Rather let us say that the moral choice is comparable to the construction of a work of art. But here I must at once digress to make it quite clear that we (existentialists) are not propounding an aesthetic morality, for our adversaries are disingenuous enough to reproach us even with that. . . . There is this in common between art and morality, that in both we have to do with creation and invention. We can not decide a priori what it is that should be done. . . . Man makes himself; he is not found ready-made; he makes himself by the choice of his morality, and he can not but choose a morality, such is the pressure of circumstances upon him. We define man only in relation to his commitments; it is therefore absurd to reproach us for irresponsibility in our choice. (Sartre quoted in Kaufmann, 364-365)

Returning to our discussion of Dostoyevsky, in his passage on the author in *The Encyclopedia of Philosophy*, Paul Edwards describes the dilemma raised by Dostoyevsky's acceptance of the notion of radical freedom and the meaninglessness of our experience in this way:

> The total freedom of the underground man brought Dostoyevsky to the total terror of a universe without truth or principle, good or evil, virtue or vice. This nihilist vision of the

universe was to send philosophers like L.I. Shestov and Nietzsche into dark ecstasy over the naked power of the will, and it
was also to bring Dostoyevsky to what seemed to be an irresolv-
able dilemma: Freedom is the supreme good because man is not
man unless he is free, but freedom is also a supreme evil because man is free to do anything, including illimitable destruc-
tion. . . . These two kinds of freedom are most fully embodied
and brought into conflict in the persons of Christ and the Grand
Inquisitor in "The Legend of the Grand Inquisitor.". . . Christ's
freedom is that of conditionless faith, given by man in fearful
and lonely anxiety and without the reassurance of rational
proof, miracles, or the support of the crowd. The freedom of the
Grand Inquisitor is the freedom of the superior will, presented
in its most attractive form. . . . So powerfully did Dostoyevsky
dramatize the Grand Inquisitor's argument against Christ and
his freedom that critical opinion has split since that time in
choosing Christ or the Grand Inquisitor as the bearer of truth.
Dostoyevsky was without doubt on the side of Christ, but he
meant to have each reader decide in free and lonely anxiety
where to place his own belief. (412)

In the same manner, Allen presents the views of the nihilist and the
believer in so powerful a fashion that it is possible to claim that he himself favors either side. Indeed, it is for this reason that Allen has so often
been accused of favoring narcissism or moral relativity. While it is clear
that this debate rages within Allen as fiercely as it did within Dostoyevsky, ultimately, in my view, Allen's own position is in accord with
the believer. Too often have we seen Allen's indictment of those who
have forgotten the values of their heritage to conclude otherwise.

Finally, it is in this scene, for the first time, that Judah is forced, by
the most powerful moral voice within him (that of his father), to face up
to the true nature of his crime by giving it the name it deserves, that of
murder!

When we next see Judah, he is in his office lying to the police detective about his knowledge and involvement with Dolores. While his lies
seem persuasive to us, Judah expresses his terror that he may have made
a slip as he talks over the incident with Jack. When he then reveals that
he has an overpowering urge to just confess and get the whole thing over
with, Jack explodes in anger urging him "to be a man," and saying that
he's not going to go to jail to satisfy Judah's sense of guilt. Judah de-

mands to know if Jack is threatening him. While Jack denies it, Judah realizes that his father was right in his claim that "one sin leads to deeper sin, adultery, fornication, lies, killing. . ." Judah now sees that the way he thought about Dolores, as a problem that could be solved by just one push of a button, could also be applied by Jack to him. In a sense, Judah's intellect leads him to use the golden rule to see the ultimate wrongness of his act. By acting to murder Dolores when she became a problem for him, Judah realizes that he intellectually gave his permission to Jack to do the same if he, Judah, becomes a similar obstacle.

* * *

The second plotline in *Crimes and Misdemeanors* is the story of Cliff Stern and his attempt to maintain his moral integrity in the face of the nihilism represented by his wife Wendy (Joanna Gleason), her brother Lester, and Halley Reed. While Wendy and Lester are Ben's siblings, they share none of his spiritual commitment. Wendy urges Cliff to made a flattering documentary of Lester, a successfully but shallow TV producer. Halley works for public television which has commissioned the show. Cliff reluctantly agrees only because he needs the money to finance his much more serious project, a film profile of the philosopher Louis Levy. As the film progresses, we learn that Cliff's marriage to Wendy is close to ending and we watch as Cliff competes with Lester for Halley's affection. Cliff's plans are destroyed when he learns that Levy has committed suicide. Shocked, Cliff sits in his office watching a videotape in which Levy expresses his views on suicide. When he finishes speaking, the video screen goes all white, almost as though an explosion had suddenly engulfed Levy. Halley appears to offer her condolences although she notes that regardless of the complexity of any philosophical system, "in the end it's got to be incomplete."

This pessimistic, and unquestionably accurate, appraisal of all philosophical systems, including those to come, leaves us with apparently few options. On the one hand, like Judah, Jack, or Lester, we can choose to base our lives solely on hedonistic principles seeking to get as much as we can for ourselves, and destroying those who get in the way. Or, like Aunt May, we can become permanent cynics, attacking everything and everyone around us while hypocritically placing all our hopes on some utopian ideology (like Marxism) which promises us salvation, either here on earth or in some mystical heaven. Or, we can take Sol's approach and choose to commit ourselves to a set of values while simultaneously acknowledging that such a choice can only be based on faith and never knowledge. Finally, we can follow Louis Levy's path and escape all of lives woes and contradictions by simply ending life.

In the last videotape we watch of Levy, he begins by echoing Camus in his suggestion that we all need to be given a reason not to commit suicide, "to persuade us to stay in life." Yet, as Cliff tells us, Levy was able to construct such a reason through the creation of his philosophy of affirmation. This positive outlook on life was enough to get him through horrendous experiences. Cliff hints, but does not actually say, that Levy's family was killed in the Holocaust, and that Levy just barely escaped with his life. Given May's earlier reference to the Holocaust as the ultimate horror, one can understand Cliff's disbelief that Levy could make it through such an experience, survive, go on to live for over forty more years, and then, suddenly, decide to take his own life.

The answer to this puzzle, like that surrounding the death of Primo Levy, the real-life figure whose story is very similar, is one which Allen never reveals, but we can speculate. Despite its overwhelming horror, in some ways the Holocaust can be intellectually dealt with if it is viewed as an aberration, a unique event perpetuated by a nation cowed by economic collapse and international humiliation, and led by a madman who ruled with an iron fist. If the Holocaust was such an aberration, detested and abhorred by all sane, right-thinking, decent people: then we can be shocked by the enormity of its evil while still remaining basically optimistic about the human condition and its future.

After all, one could argue, the world did eventually crush Nazism, and when the true scope of the Holocaust became known, the international community agreed to hold war crimes trials at Nuremberg at which the remaining architects of the killing were tried, convicted, and executed. Today, only a very small number of crackpots, with no real clout, continue to defend the Nazis; and even most of those fanatics base their defense on the obviously erroneous claim that the Holocaust did not actually occur. By making such a claim, no matter how hypocritically, they admit openly that had the Holocaust in fact taken place, even they would be forced to admit that it was wrong.

Addressing May's other implicit point, namely the question as to how God could have stood by and allowed the Holocaust to take place without intervening, theologians have had an answer to this kind of question for centuries. Because it is essential to God that we humans possess the free will to choose between good and evil, He leaves it to us to decide when to resist the evil of others. It was once only the Jewish people who agreed to follow Moses and make the many sacrifices required to reach the promised land. God sent the miracles which helped pave their way to the Exodus. And, even with God's miracles, the Egyptians were not convinced to allow the Jews to go; right until the end they pursued their former slaves until finally, with the miracle of the parting of the waves, they were destroyed.

In a similar fashion, a theologian could argue that the Holocaust was perpetuated by free individuals who chose to obey the immoral commands of their leaders when they could have done otherwise. Eventually, because so many around the world freely chose to risk their lives to oppose this evil, it was destroyed. Such a theologian could even argue that God may in fact have intervened miraculously in the conflict in ways that are clear for those who wish to see them. Again and again, one could argue, the Allies were helped by accidents, discoveries, and mistakes in strategy on the other side which some could call "miracles." Indeed, if, at the beginning of the Battle of Britain, you had told most people that in a mere five years the Axis would be completely defeated and Hitler dead, they would have be willing to call such an outcome a "miracle."

But none of this answers our question. If in fact Levy was able to survive the Holocaust with his optimism intact, then what could have occurred in the intervening years to destroy his spirit and lead him to suicide? The answer to this question is hinted at in Allen's portrayal of the character Frederick in his 1984 film *Hannah and her Sisters*. Frederick is a man who has experienced the meaninglessness of life and the terror of dread. Rather than persevere, he has given up the search in order to inhabit an sterile abyss of his own making, one of loneliness, bitterness, and frustration. He is filled with hatred for the hypocrisy around him and he expresses it in a compelling soliloquy.

For Frederick, the Holocaust is not the unique aberration of which we spoke, but instead simply an exaggeration of the way we regularly treat each other more and more in our contemporary world. Like Allen himself, Frederick is convinced that the evil of the Holocaust is symptomatic of a fundamental degradation of the human spirit which is progressing at a frighteningly rapid pace in a world in which everyone is increasing motivated by a hedonistic self-interest, and all references to morality are taken to be either the ravings of pompous frauds or the sighs of hopelessly naive innocents who have blinded themselves to the operation of the "real world" all around them.

Louis Levy finally realized this truth, the ultimate extension of Hannah Arendt's famous description of "the banality of evil," and, being a fundamentally honest person, concluded that nothing he could say or do would stop this degradation and, additionally, that he no longer wished to live in such a world. Given the complete pessimism of such a conclusion, he had nothing more to say, so in his note he simply reported his decision.

* * *

To make matters worse for Cliff, Halley rejects his romantic advances in order to travel to England on business. She tells him that they will resolve the issues in their relationship when she returns. Cliff compares this postponement to serving a jail sentence. To emphasize this metaphor, we see Cliff and his niece Jenny (Jenny Nichols) at the movies watching an old prison film, *The Last Gangster* (1937), in which Edward G. Robinson serves out a term as stylized titles show the months passing. Allen then cleverly uses a similar title to tell us that Cliff's sentence has now passed as he shows us the exterior of the hotel where the wedding reception for Ben's daughter is being held. Thus, the film is given a certain symmetry in that it begins and ends at public celebrations.

Ben, wearing dark sunglasses which suggest that he is now completely blind, is surrounded by guests who must be identified for him by his wife. We see Cliff and Wendy making their way through the guests as Cliff complains that everything he's wearing is rented and Wendy responds by asking him if they can get along at this, the last event connected to her family, which they will have to attend together. Clearly, Cliff has fulfilled the task assigned him by Halley and is on the verge of being free to pursue their aborted romance. Judah and Miriam are also present. We see Judah pat Ben reassuringly on the arm as he tells Judah how happy he is that he is there.

Cliff tells his sister how his breakup with Wendy has saddened him despite its inevitability and jokes about how long he's gone without sex. Judah, on the other hand, seems to have overcome his depression. We see him celebrating with Miriam as his daughter Sharon (Stephanie Roth) tells her fiancee Chris (Gregg Edelman) that she expects him to get drunk and then argue with Ben about God. She also jokingly points out the similarities between Judah's attitudes and those of his Aunt May.

We see Cliff standing uncomfortably as two women praise Lester for paying for his niece's wedding because, we assume, the now blind Ben is out of work and without an income. Suddenly, Cliff gets a shocked look on his face and begins to move slowly away from the talk-

ing women and towards the entrance of the reception hall. Cliff is horrified to see Halley all dressed up (and without her glasses), as she stands
with an exuberant Lester. As Cliff stares at her grimly, Halley, and then
Lester, greet him happily and we overhear Lester introducing Halley as
his fiancée.

Halley's betrayal tops all of the past betrayals of Allen's earlier
films. Her lack of glasses suggests that she has overcome whatever earlier moral standards she might have had, and Lester's comments about
the caviar confirm our suspicion that Halley is marrying Lester primarily
for his wealth and fame, as well as the career opportunities he can create
for her. In this sense, Halley's betrayal is Allen's most offensive in that
she betrays not only Cliff but herself. If we assume that she ultimately
shares Cliff's opinion of Lester, and that she was starting to fall for Cliff
when she left for London, then she has chosen to sell her soul (just as
Judah did) for the sake of material success. Earlier, Judah quoted Sol as
saying that each little sin leads to deeper ones. Halley's misdemeanors
are different from Judah's crime only in degree, not in kind.

The wedding ceremony now seems to mock Cliff as we see him sitting in the same row with Lester, Halley, and Wendy. Still shocked, he
glances towards Halley in dismay but she ignores him. After the ceremony, Halley approaches Cliff as he drinks alone in an alcove. She tries
to convince Cliff that Lester is really a wonderful man, but Cliff refuses
to listen. When Halley asks him to give her a little credit, he responds, "I
always did before today." She then returns his one love letter to her. Like
Louis Levy, Cliff realizes that he really doesn't have any more to say. By
her actions, Halley has demonstrated what kind of person she is and Cliff
now has no interest in her. He shows his disdain by slipping into his im-
personal comic persona joking about the contents of his letter. When
Halley says she hopes that they will always remain friends, we don't
have to see Cliff's face to know his reaction, his silence speaks volumes.

An unidentified man is shown dancing Russian-style to the band's
loud music until he pulls a muscle in his leg. Two children are shown
stealing bits of icing from the uncut wedding cake. Feeling the need to
escape these antics, Judah slips down a hallway for a cigarette and encounters Cliff sitting alone and drinking on a piano bench in near darkness. Judah immediately starts talking to Cliff as though they are old
acquaintances, even though we haven't been given any indication up to
this point that they even knew each other.

As Judah tells Cliff his story, the scene shifts and we see Lester and
Wendy happily discussing the fact that she's met someone new and the
irritating Cliff will soon be out of both of their lives. We then return to the

conversation between Judah and Cliff. In it Judah, in effect, tells the only partially comprehending Cliff a "chilling story" of an unpunished contract murder, presumably his own eradicating of Dolores.

Miriam comes upon them and tells Judah that they ought to be getting home. Judah jumps up and says goodbye to Cliff ("Nice talking to you, good luck to you!"). Happily, Judah puts his arm around Miriam's shoulder as he tells her that they must plan a wedding like this for Sharon. Miriam tells him how happy he has made her tonight, and we see them stop and kiss as the sounds of the romantic song "I'll Be Seeing You" begin to swell up around them.

For many film-goers, this pessimistic exchange is the last scene of which they are aware. When we see the blind Ben dancing with his daughter followed by a montage of earlier scenes from the film, many in the audience probably start rustling in their seats and preparing to leave the theater. However, those willing to stay, and able to hear over the sounds of departure around them, and the music coming from the screen, are presented with the narration from Louis Levy with which our discussion of this film began.

If one accepts my optimistic reading of the end of Levy's narration, then, at the film's conclusion, Cliff may be down but he is not out. He has maintained his integrity and, in this sense, still has a genuine chance to construct a fulfilling life by pursuing the very goals (family and work), which, Levy tells us, are the fundamental ingredients for a joyous life.

Further, despite Judah's assertions to the contrary, it is not at all clear that he has really escaped from the deep sense of guilt within him. If he had, then why would he have indiscreetly told Cliff, a virtual stranger, so accurate a version of his story? Obviously, if Cliff thinks about what he was told, he might very well come to realize later the significance of Judah's "murder story." The details of what Judah told him would be easy enough to check: the trip to Europe with his family, the recent murder of one of his patients about which Judah was questioned by the police, the conviction of a another man for the crime who had also been found guilty of other murders. While it may be unlikely that Cliff will be the one to investigate Judah's "story," there is no reason for us to think that Judah won't repeat this incident again and again, telling strangers his murder plot every time he's had too many to drink until, eventually, he is taken seriously.

And, even if this doesn't happen (Judah would tell me I've seen too many movies), it is clear that Judah is lying, especially to himself, when he claims to have overcome his guilt. His life will always be tainted by his crime. While he might be able to force himself to pretend to enjoy his wealth and security, he admitted to Cliff that he is just rationalizing. Given what we have seen of his character, it is more likely that his high spirits at the film's end are temporary, and that, in the long run, he will secretly torment himself for the rest of his life. In addition, we know that Judah can not truly take pleasure from the primary source of human joy which Levy mentions, that of family. He can't find joy in his family because he ultimately realizes, no matter how hard he tries to hide the truth from himself, that with them he wears a mask, he inauthentically hides his true nature.

How could he find joy in a relationship with a woman who bores him, whose idea of a birthday present is a treadmill? We know now that Judah is a sensitive and passionate person. How long will it be before he tires of the endless empty chatter of his home life and his wife's desire to constantly entertain guests whom he finds shallow and frivolous? He is trapped in a loveless marriage to a person who doesn't realize how lonely he really is. When he arranged to have Delores killed, he destroyed any chance of beginning again authentically. His fate will now be more like that of the characters of Sartre's *No Exit*, doomed to spend eternity in relationships with those who can only serve as his tormentors.

In the end, Judah has failed to fulfill the obligations imposed on him by his father when Sol named him after the great Jewish leader Judah Maccabee. Instead of defending the values of his heritage against the pagan hedonism of those who wished to oppress his people, this latter-day Judah has betrayed all for the sake of a material wealth which, in the long run, means very little to him.

However, Allen himself denies this interpretation. In his written interview with me, Allen says, "You are wrong about Judah, he feels no guilt and the extremely rare time the events occur to him, his mild uneasiness (which sometimes doesn't come at all) is negligible" (374). While the reader is free to accept Allen's response as the final word on this point, I would argue that the film's text gives stronger support to my interpretation. How could I possibly claim to have greater insight into Judah's character than his creator? I would contend that in many instances artists do not possess privileged access to all of the nuances of their creations. Ernest Hemingway was famous for denying symbolic meanings in his novels which were obvious to his readers. Allen acknowledges that his audience may on occasion understand his work even better than himself when he tells me in our interview that, "Louis Levy was related to Primo Levy only unconsciously. I wasn't aware of the similarity in name 'til long after the picture was out and someone pointed it out to me. I'm very aware of Levi's writing and he is probably present on an unconscious level" (374).

Ultimately, I think Allen wants each of us to make our own decisions about the film's meaning. He wants to affect us, to shock us so that we will each leave the theater thinking seriously about these issues, something we would be less likely to do if he had provided us with Cliff's more traditional Hollywood ending.

It is appropriate that the film end with a shot of Ben. It is only by blinding ourselves to the "truth" of the "real world" that one can create a meaningful and fulfilling life. If the universe is fundamentally indifferent to our human capacity to love and create meaning for our lives, then we have absolutely no reason for choosing a truth which only destroys life's joy. In this sense, Sol is right when he proclaims that, "If necessary, I will always choose God over truth!"

It is true, as some critics of the film maintain, that Allen presents us with no compelling arguments to persuade us of the validity of Ben and Sol's position over that of Jack and Judah. The reason for this, I have argued, is that Allen believes that it would be a violation of his integrity as an artist, and of his deeply-held position as an existentialist, if he were to suggest that an objective ground for ethics exists when he has himself been unable to discover such a ground.

And yet, Allen's conscience requires him to argue for adherence to some form of moral structure. Admittedly, the moral code which he proposes in his films is open to many criticisms. Allen makes it quite clear that those who choose the path of morality are by no means assured of a happier or a more successful life than those who choose the path of hedonism. Again and again in his films, he shows us characters who choose morality over self-interest only to end up worse off than those who strive solely for success. To an Aunt May, Cliff Stern is no more than one of life's losers; yet, Allen clearly believes, by adhering to standards of personal honor and integrity he is living a much more meaningful life than those who, like Lester, Jack, and Judah, have traded their souls for material success and the satisfaction of their senses.

Allen can not prove to us that we ought to act morally. Indeed, his despair derives from his recognition that all empirical evidence seems to confirm the claim of one of his characters in Allen's earlier film *September* (1987) that the universe is "haphazard and unimaginably violent." And yet, like Soloveichik's Adam the second, Allen can not resist the spiritual impulses within himself. On those occasions when he allows himself the indulgence of faith, he chooses to believe in a moral structure which justifies and rewards the sacrifices it demands by instilling a sense of righteousness which is much more precious than material success.

Allen allows Sol to acknowledge that even if he knew with certainty that his faith was false, that the universe was truly hollow, he would still choose to believe rather than betray the only values upon which a meaningful life may be constructed.

There is no way to predict where Allen's internal struggle will finally lead him. Perhaps the character who best symbolizes this struggle is Louis Levy, the philosopher whose faith and strength of will were strong enough to survive the Holocaust and to create an optimistic existential philosophy. Levy may have been driven by despair to commit suicide midway through *Crimes and Misdemeanors*, yet, at the film's conclusion, he is miraculously resurrected as the spokesperson for a bittersweet moral optimism which is able to proclaim that "most human beings seem to have the ability to keep trying, and even to find joy, from simple things like the family, their work, and from the hope that future generations might understand more." Perhaps someday Allen will be able to celebrate Levy's faith without also feeling the obligation to share in his despair.

Bibliography

Allen, Woody. *Getting Even*. New York: Random House, 1971.
———. Side Effects. New York: Random House, 1980.
———. Without Feathers. New York: Random House, 1975.
Barrett, William. *Irrational Man: A Study in Existential Philosophy*. New York: Anchor, 1962.
Becker, Ernest. *The Denial of Death*. New York: The Free Press, 1973.
Brode, Douglas. *The Films of Woody Allen: Revised and Updated*. Secaucus, New Jersey: Citadel Press, 1991.
Buber, Martin. *I and Thou*. Translated by Walter Kaufmann. New York: Charles Scribner's Sons, 1970.
Camus, Albert. *The Myth of Sisyphus and other essays*. Translated by Justin O'Brien. New York: Vintage International, 1983.
Dostoevsky, Fyodor. *Crime and Punishment*. Translated by Constance Garnett. New York: Random House,1956.
———. *The Brothers Karamozov*. Translated by Constance Garnett. New York: Heritage Press,1949.
Edwards, Paul, ed. *The Encyclopedia of Philosophy*. 8 vols. New York: Macmillan Publishing Co., 1972.
Girgus, Sam B. *The Films of Woody Allen*. New York: Cambridge University Press, 1993.

Hirsch, Foster. *Love, Sex, Death, and the Meaning of Life*. New York: McGraw-Hill Paperbacks, 1981.

Jacobs, Diane. . . . *but we need the eggs: The Magic of Woody Allen*. New York: St. Martin's Press, 1982.

Kaufmann, Walter, ed. *Existentialism from Dostoevsky to Sartre*. New York: Meridian, 1975.

Lax, Eric. *Woody Allen: A Biography*. New York: Vintage Books, 1992.

Lee, Sander. *Woody Allen's Angst: Philosophical Commentaries on his Serious Films*. Jefferson, North Carolina: McFarland Publishing Co., 1997.

Nietzsche, Frederick. *Thus Spake Zarathustra*. Translated by Walter Kaufmann. New York: Penguin Books, 1978.

Oaklander, L. Nathan. *Existentialist Philosophy: An Introduction*. 2nd ed. Upper Saddle River, New Jersey: Prentice Hall, 1996.

Olafson, Frederick. *Persons and Principles: An Ethical Interpretation of Existentialism*. Baltimore, Maryland: Johns Hopkins Press, 1967.

Plato. The Republic. Translated by Desmond Lee. New York: Penguin Books, 1983.

Pogel, Nancy. Woody Allen. Boston, Massachuetts: Twayne Publishers, 1987.

Sartre, Jean-Paul. *Being and Nothingness*. Translated by Hazel Barnes. New York: Washington Square Press, 1971.

———. *The Emotions: Outline of a Theory*. Translated by Bernard Frechtman. New York: Philosophical Library, 1948.

———. *Existentialism and Humanism*. London: Methuen and Company, 1948.

———. *Imagination: A Psychological Critique*. Translated by Forrest Williams. Ann Arbor, Michigan: The University of Michigan Press, 1962.

———. *Nausea*. Translated by Lloyd Alexander. New York: New Directions Publishing Co., 1964.

———. *No Exit and Three Other Plays*. Translated by Lionel Abel. New York: Vintage International, 1989.

———. *"What is Literature?" and other essays*. Cambridge, Massachuetts: Harvard University Press, 1988.

Soloveitchik, Joseph B. *The Lonely Man of Faith*. New York: Doubleday Dell Publishing Group, 1992.

Yacowar, Maurice. *Loser Take All: The Comic Art of Woody Allen*. New Expanded Edition. New York: Continuum, Frederick Unger Publishing Co.,1991.

Dissonant Harmonies
Classical Music and the Problems of Class in
Crimes and Misdemeanors

THOMAS FAHY

As a jazz clarinetist, director, and writer, Woody Allen listens carefully to the ways music can enhance the thematic and emotive content of his films. His deliberate selection of pieces suggests that music is essential to understanding his works more fully. While most critics and viewers would agree that jazz plays an integral role in his films, the intention behind his sparing use of classical music also deserves serious examination.[1] *Crimes and Misdemeanors* (1989),[2] in particular, invites us to savor both what we see and what we hear. Alongside a world of black evening gowns, expensive cars, and stunning parties is the lyricism of Franz Schubert, while Johann Sebastian Bach accompanies philosophical insights and intellectual savvy. Classical music,[3] in other words, reinforces class distinctions that define its characters and present cultured knowledge as essential for access to upper-class and intellectual communities. For Judah Rosenthal (Martin Landau), understanding the differences between Schubert and Schumann reflects his superior intellectual and social standing and, in part, justifies his ultimate rejection of working-class Dolores (Anjelica Huston)æthe flight attendant with whom he has had a two-year affair. Bach's music emphasizes Professor Louis Levy's (Martin Bergmann) place in the ivory tower of academia, undermining the legitimacy of his philosophical insights about "real life." Since most of the audience does not belong to either of these worlds, feeling a bit like Cliff (Woody Allen) who rents a tux to formal events, this distance enables us to remain somewhat critical of the ways class identities (wealth and intellect) can become justifications for selfishness and cruelty.

While we typically expect classical music to be linked with elitism, it also bridges class barriers between audience and characters in this film. Its absence, in contexts where we would expect it, invites viewers to sympathize with Judah and Levy, and, more specifically, to ignore what we know about them. We like Judah, in part, because we enjoy looking at him: his beautiful things, stable family, and successful career. We also revel in the thought of being profound and esteemed like Levy. Although part of this appeal lies in the knowledge (of medicine, music, and books) which defines them as intellectuals, their knowledge is surprisingly understated; it does not get presented in ways that would isolate them significantly from the audience. Judah never talks of his work or plays music, for example; and Levy does not discuss his life as an academic. This essay specifically examines the ways classical music both defines characters by class and minimizes these differences in order to elicit sympathy. More specifically, the absence of classical music in certain personal spaces (Judah's living room and Levy's office) has the effect of leveling class distinctions between audience and characters. As we find ourselves willing to see crimes as misdemeanors, we identify with Judah and Levyæseeing their personal struggles with fidelity, greed, and/or suicide as universal. Unable to judge them too severely, our sympathetic responses contribute to the moral ambiguity of the film. In this way, music ultimately becomes a moral signifier that offers us the type of structure and balanceæthe ability to accept both right and wrongæthat continually seems to allude these characters.

Death and the Maiden

During the opening dinner celebrating Judah's invaluable contributions to a new ophthalmology wing, the master of ceremonies praises him not in terms of medicine, but in terms of culture: "You can also call Judah to find out about which is the best restaurant in Paris or Athens, or which hotel to stay at in Moscow, or the best recording of a particular Mozart symphony." Exotic travels, elegant restaurants, and high-caliber music distinguish the upper class from the rest of society. And Judah embodies the best characteristics of this world. Classical music not only contributes to other people's perception of him as "superior," but it also highlights the class barriers undermining his relationship with Dolores. To some extent, Dolores believes that love and passion can shatter the social proprieties and affectations keeping them apart. By demanding to speak with Judah's wife Miriam (Claire Bloom), Dolores wants to make their clandestine relationship real, seeking public or external acknowledgement as both a means of validating their love and transcending class. Her recollection of an earlier assignation at the beach, however, suggests that such transcendence is not possible: .

> J (after kissing on the beach): "I'm feeling self-conscious."
> D: "Let's go back to the cottage and light a fire, and you can play me the Schumann."
> J: "Schu*bert*. Schumann is flowery. Schubert is . . . he reminds me of you . . . the sad one."
> D: "Schubert. You have to teach me all that. I'm so ignorant in classical music."
> J: "I'll teach you. Someday we'll have a lot of time."

Dolores views classical music as a type of privileged knowledge that creates an imbalance in their relationship. The ability to distinguish between Schubert and Schumann identifies Judah's sophistication, worldliness, and class; whereas, this lack in Dolores places her in an inferior intellectual and social category. This imbalance also introduces another barrier by suggesting a student/teacher relationship between them. Dolores is never presented as having something new or valuable to offer Judah; she forever remains the sad, dutiful student who gives him Schubert recordings for his birthday and waits for him to actæout of love instead of class difference.

Dolores' mistaken reference to Schumann also suggests biographical connections between her and the composer. Schumann suffered from manic depression, a bipolar affective disorder, and numerous physical disorders throughout his life, and his first breakdown occurred as early as 1833.[4] After attempting suicide in 1854, he sought psychiatric care at a hospital. His friends and family had witnessed a gradual mental deterioration for years, and a number of his late compositions were criticized and dismissed by musicians (including his wife) who considered them to be products of an unstable mind. Ironically, Dolores is the one who mentions Schumann, a connection that Judah desperately does not want to see. He dismisses the composer's music as "flowery" because this allusion adds to his culpability in her emotional and psychological breakdown; she is presented as smoking, shaking, screaming, drinking, popping pills, and crying because of their deteriorating relationship. When confiding in his patient Ben (Sam Waterston) about the affair, Judah eventually describes her as "unstable," "hysteric," and "vindictive." The film, however, never offers a perspective that would validate or explain any of her actions. Instead, this characterization ultimately gives Judah—and the audience—a way to accept her murder. She is objectified and constructed as a volatile problem, not a person. The connection between Dolores and Schumann, therefore, complicates our moral responses to this affair because it asks us to see Judah as burdened by her instability. Through her frantic attempts to expose their relationship with late-night phone calls and letters, for example, Dolores is clearly dangerous. She also knows more that Judah realizes. And by seeing through his self-righteous excuses, she can expose the lies, deceptions, and licentiousness underneath upper-class masks of social propriety and morality.

Eventually, Dolores tries to use both Judah's misappropriation of hospital funds and his interest in Schubert to legitimize their relationship. Public exposure of Judah's financial indiscretions would ruin his place in the upper-class world he has built for himself and his family, and Judah cannot let this happen. Up until this point in the film, he has dismissed her claims of personal, emotional, and financial sacrifices for him, arguing that there were "no business opportunities" and "no lovers begging for your hand"; "it's all in your head!" By reducing her claims to intangible fantasies, he continues to make their relationship invisible to the world outside her apartment—a place that had become his sanctuary from both class distinctions and marital responsibility. She responds, however, with the implied threat of blackmail and by giving him a recording of Schubert's music for his birthday—both tangible things which force Judah to recognize that she has been a significant part of his life for over two years. Dolores' gift suggests that she has gained some understanding of classical music. She gives him Schubert, not Schumann or any other composer, because Judah thought Schubert's music was both better and like her. In effect, she co-opts Schubert though a gift that will make Judah associate his music with her. This act of reclaiming Schubert in her own terms also breaks down class barriers. Knowledge of classical music has been one of the qualities defining Judah as part of the upper class, but her understanding of it brings her dangerously close to his world.

Schubert's String Quartet in G major (D. 887, 1826) plays during two scenes that both underscore the class division defining their relationship and accentuate the moral tension surrounding her murder. In general, even though the quartet is in a major key, Schubert alters the third in the first full measure of the first movement to begin with a strong, dramatic statement in G minor (B natural becomes B-flat). He plays with the tension between major and minor throughout the work, and even in the closing measures G major and G minor battle for harmonic dominance. This tension seems to parallel Judah's personal and moral struggles in deciding to have Dolores killed—choosing between right/wrong, justice/lawlessness, middle-class/upper-class, and major/minor. The quartet first plays when the killer parks his car and follows Dolores along a busy street to her small apartment. At the same time, we see Judah's spacious living room—the warm fireplace, the countless books—and his family is arguing about whether his daughter's honeymoon should be in Italy or Australia. Not only do these homes reflect their different places in society, but this juxtaposition also presents the upper class as a secluded place of security. In its clean, open spaces, the Rosenthal's seems honest and good. Dolores, however, lives behind locked doors which must be opened with keys or security buzzers. In her world, which is much darker and more confined, terrible things can happen.

Schubert's G major quartet also reinforces the class barrier between Judah and his brother Jack (Jerry Orbach) and presents immoral decisions as part of everyday existence. Throughout the film, each discussion between the brothers reveals a long-lasting rift in their relationship involving money, status, attitudes about life, and morality. Acutely aware of these differences, Judah knows the possible solutions Jack will offer when he confides in him about Dolores and his "financial indiscretion." Yet Judah initially gives a class-conditioned response to Jack's suggestions of violence and murder—outrage and shock being appropriate reactions from those who perceive themselves as upright. When Judah suggests moral indignation to the thought of murder, Jack immediately sees through this affectation: "You're not aware of what goes on in this world. You sit up here with your four acres and your country club and your rich friends . . . . I'm not so high-class that I can avoid looking at reality." Jack pinpoints the artificiality of upper-class society, suggesting that their sense morality is disingenuous. It exists for show, not any legitimate sense of justice. Unlike Judah, he also recognizes that a distinct class system divides America. For both the brothers, killing Dolores is a practical solution, but at the same time, Judah cannot see himself on the same level with the class of people that Jack and Dolores represent. After the murder, Judah goes to Dolores' apartment to steal evidence that would link him to her, and Schubert's quartet accompanies images of her body, her blood, and her open, staring eyes. On one hand, classical music reinforces the rift between what Judah is (a murderer), how he wants others to see him (a just, upper-class aesthete and gentleman), and how he sees his brother (also a murderer). On the other hand, Schubert's association with the crime suggests for the audience that the brothers are very much the same (they're both killers), with one difference. Jack can look crimes in the face; his brother cannot. Judah needs to preserve an upper-class life that enables him to remain aloof and conveniently naïve—unaffected by crime, violence, and exposure.

Ivory Towers

Classical music also points to the artificiality and hypocrisy of academic circles, which can be as equally exclusive and immoral as upper-class society. Louis Levy is a stereotypical professor—dedicated to an intellectual life, surrounded by faded books in a drab office, walking down icy pathways on a university campus, and wearing bland, unimaginative outfits. During each filmed interview, we hear the Prelude from Bach's English Suite in A minor (BWV 807, circa 1720). As with Judah, recurring classical music helps define Levy as being part of an exclusive world. Bach typically used and expanded sophisticated and systematic musical forms (such as preludes, fugues, and dances), and, in part, this highly complex and contrapuntal composition mirrors Levy's intellectualism. The prelude of the suite opens like a fugue with a motivic statement in A minor and a response on the dominant (E major)—the intricate counterpoint and quick tempo working contrapuntally with Levy's slow, accented speech. These elements, along with the label "professor," lend his ideas and thoughts immediate authority and respectability. In other words, we privilege his ideas by placing them in a certain class—that of the intellectual—a class which Bach's music subtly reinforces.

Nevertheless, Levy's suicide, and to a lesser extent the music accompanying his interviews, ultimately undermine his life-affirming philosophies about love and relationships, therefore suggesting the artificiality of the intellectual class. Just as the minor key of Bach's English Suite foreshadows the professor's tragic end, this music helps situate Levy as part of class that is equally disconnected from middle-class reality (as represented by Cliff). For most of the film, the association of Bach—and classical music more broadly—with esoteric intellectualism creates a certain distance between Levy and the audience. Levy, for example, seems to be part of a stodgy, uninteresting academic world when juxtaposed with Bach's lively music. In order to find value in his philosophies, we must ultimately move beyond his identity as a professor and the pessimism of his selfish, cowardly act of suicide. Sander H. Lee interprets Levy's suicide in terms of disillusionment: Levy may have survived the Holocaust, but "being a fundamentally honest person he . . . concluded that nothing he could say or do would stop [the fundamental degradation of the human spirit] and . . . he no longer wished to live in such a world. Given the complete pessimism of such a conclusion, he had nothing more to say, so in his note he simply reported his decision" (281). We can also read Levy's last words—"I've gone out the window"—as speaking to the moral and social failures of intellectual life; he abandons a world where words do not have the power to change things, only actions do. The references to Bach's music also die with him, for after his death, we no longer hear any classical music.

Silencing the Music

Even though classical music is a formal art form that carries connotations of elitism, *Crimes and Misdemeanors* creates an intimate relationship among the audience, Judah, and to some degree, Levy. On one level, the fallibility of these characters helps us move past our negative assumptions about upper-class wealth, refined tastes, and intellectualism. Self-doubts, morality, and questions about faith plague Judah; clearly the trappings of success and refinement have not freed him from suffering and doubt. And these ongoing struggles elicit our sympathy. The absence of classical music at certain points also seems to reinforce our willingness to forgive Judah, or at least to minimize the severity of what he has done. With the number of references to classical music in this film, we would expect to see Judah either listening to a Mozart Concerto in his office, car, or living room, or playing a Chopin Nocturne at a piano. However, we never actually hear classical music in any of these places; the warm living room and fireplace, to which the film so often returns, keeps us on intimate, less formal terms with him. It is a space without music. As a matter of fact, he is only associated with classical music intellectually, not literally. By minimizing the tangible role of classical music, the film makes it easier for middle-class audiences to relate to him—to see themselves in him and find ways to overlook what he has done to Dolores. We envy his knowledge and money because we want what these things symbolize—success and intelligence. And our empathy is contingent on not feeling excluded from this world.

In a similar fashion, we must separate the message from the messenger in order to extract something positive from Levy words; and Allen achieves this by removing Levy's image and Bach's music from the epilogue:

> We are all faced throughout our lives with agonizing decisions,
> moral choices. Some are on a grand scale; most of these choices
> are on lesser points, but we define ourselves by the choices we
> have made. We are, in fact, the sum-total of our choices. Events
> unfold so unpredictably, so unfairly, human happiness does not
> seem to have been included in the design of creation. It is only
> we, with our capacity to love, that give meaning to the indiffer-
> ent universe. And yet, most human beings seem to have the abil-
> ity to keep trying, and even to find joy from simple things like
> their family, their work, and from the hope that future genera-
> tions might understand more.

Hope can only be found in these words by denying what we know. As
Judah tells Cliff at the end of the film, "In reality, we rationalize, we deny
or we couldn't go on living." We too must forget the professor has killed
himself and Judah has gotten away with murder. In other words, we must
abandon our moral judgements of these acts to find something meaningful. The impact of Levy's words comes in part from the fact that he is no
longer associated with an esoteric, intellectual world; we no longer see
any images of him as a professor.

For the first time, Bach, who has functioned as a leitmotif for Levy,
is not being played while the professor speaks; instead, an instrumental
version of the song "I'll Be Seeing You" (Fain, 1938) accompanies the
final montage and image of Ben dancing with his daughter. The combination of these images with sentimental music gives the end of the film
an unexpected, bitter-sweet quality. We get caught up in the nostalgic
recollections of the story in spite of what the characters have done.
Specifically, this change in music shifts our attitude about what Levy
says by allowing us to disassociate his words from his actions. After his
death, we no longer link him to an aloof, intellectual class, but with a
tune we can sing and dance to. His words now speak to a much broader
audience because images of his status as professor and the complexities
of Bach's music are gone. It is the shift from classical to jazz, from intellect to emotion, that helps make Levy's words more universal. Nostalgia
is not rational; it reminds us of a past that we have idealized in order to
feel good about ourselves. Like the closing montage, the song only recalls a catalogue of pleasant memories and clichés: "I'll be seeing you in
all the old familiar places . . . that small café, the park across the way, the
children's carousel, the chestnut trees, the wishing well." Ultimately, this
ending asks us to reject the intellect for nostalgia, to think with our hearts
instead of our minds, and to be accepting instead of judgmental. Levy

has done this, becoming so heartsick that he kills himself. His words have amounted to nothing, so his heart makes a decision to end it all. But just as the intellect fails for Levy, his nostalgia has failed to leave him any life-affirming choices.

Cadences

Our conflicted relationship to Judah and Levy (our fondness for Judah and our desire to find affirmation in Levy's words) points to the moral ambiguity at the heart of the film—an ambiguity reinforced by classical music. This music helps establish the classes defining these characters and motivating their drastic actions. Whether it is Judah's upper-class society or Levy's academic world of thoughts and words, classical music fortifies the barriers that separate the working middle classes from these circles. At the same time, the surprising absence of this music in particular contexts erodes the boundaries separating us from them. We become increasingly intimate and forgiving of these men as Schubert and Bach fade away. Ultimately, like music itself, our willingness to compromise our own morality has to do with timing. Woody Allen brings us in and out of this story when we are most vulnerable. We see Judah struggle, suffer, and almost lose everything; we hear the richness of Levy's insight against Lester's (Alan Alda) absurd ideas about comedy and art. But what about the rest of the story? Judah's version for Cliff suggests another source for our sympathy:

> He finds that he's plagued by deep-rooted guilt . . . . He imagines that God is watching his every move. Suddenly, it's not an empty universe at all, but a just and moral one, and he's violated it. Now he's panic-stricken. He's on the verge of a mental collapse . . . and then one morning he awakens. The sun is shining and his family is around him, and, mysteriously, the crisis has lifted. He takes his family on a vacation to Europe, and, as the months pass, he finds he's not punished; in fact, he prospers. The killing gets attributed to another person. . . . His life is completely back to normal, back to his protected world of wealth and privilege.

Through images of bright sunny days and trips to Europe, Judah embraces a nostalgic vision of the past, continually denying his actions and their impact on his psyche. And this haunting statement about his return to a "protected world of wealth and privilege" raises the question: what would be different if we had witnessed this part of the story? How much longer would we sympathize with him, or believe in Levy's words? Without any conclusion, we can remain ambiguous, and the film can ask us to think about these questions over and over again. We don't think their actions are right. But like Levy and Judah, we often fail to live up to our own ideals about life and morality. Sometimes, the heroes don't win; the bad go unpunished. We are left with harmonies that do not cadence, and it is at these moments—waiting and listening for resolution—that we are most forgiving.

Notes

1. Although most critics agree that music plays a crucial role in Allen's films, classical music is never discussed in any detail; certainly, its sophisticated use in *Crimes and Misdemeanors* has been largely ignored.

2. Plot synopsis: At the outset of *Crimes and Misdemeanors*, Judah Rosenthal ends his two-year affair with Dolores Paley. Her increasing demands make him realize that his actions have jeopardized his twenty-five year marriage and successful career as a doctor. Dolores specifically threatens to confront his wife and possibly expose his illegal, financial dealings with hospital funds. After he decides to have her killed, his life-long struggles with Judaism reach a crisis when he is not "punished" by God. He returns to a life of privilege, and this condirms his worst fears that there is no God. At the same time, the sub-plot features Cliff, an independent filmmaker whose marriage is deteriorating. Having given up on his wife, he falls in love with Halley, but both of these relationships fall apart by the end of the film. Meanwhile, he is being paid to make a documentary of his brother-in-law, a rich, sleazy filmmaker named Lester. This job takes away from his personal project of interviewing Professor Levy. Levy's suicide, however, temporarily shatters Cliff's faith in human love and dignity.

3. I use the term "classical music" throughout this essay as a convenient was to label Allen's use of Baroque music (Bach) and Romantic music (Schubert and Schumann). In the context of this essay and for the

purposes of my argument, the distinction between Baroque, Classical, and Romantic music are not significant.

4. See Peter Ostwald's *Schumann: The Inner Voices of a Musical Genius.*

Works Cited

Blake, Richard A. *Woody Allen: Profane and Sacred.* Lanham, Md.: Scarecrow Press Inc., 1995.

Girgus, Sam B. *The Films of Woody Allen.* Cambridge: Cambridge University Press, 1993.

Kramer, Lawrence. *Franz Schubert: Sexuality, Subjectivity, Song.* Cambridge: Cambridge University Press, 1998.

Lee, Sander H. *Woody Allen's Angst: Philosophical Commentaries on His Serious Films.* Chapel Hill: University of North Carolina, 1997.

Minowitz, Peter. "Crimes and Controversies: Nihilism from Machiavelli to Woody Allen." *Film/Literature Quarterly* 19.2 (1991): 77–88.

Ostwald, Peter. *Schumann: The Inner Voices of a Musical Genius.* Boston: Northeastern University Press, 1985.

Quattrocchi, Edward. "Allen's Literary Antecedents in *Crimes and Misdemeanors.*" *Films/Literature Quarterly* 19.2 (1991): 90–98.

"Some of Us Are Real, Some Are Not"
Purple Rose of Cairo

WILLIAM HUTCHINGS

The first American novel about the alluring effects of Hollywood movies on the everyday lives of ordinary people was Harry Leon Wilson's *Merton of the Movies*, a popular success in 1922 that was adapted into a hit comedy on Broadway by George S. Kaufman and Marc Connelly the same year; the film version, directed by James Cruse, was released in 1924. Described by Gertrude Stein in *Everybody's Autobiography* a decade later as "the best book about twentieth-century American youth that has yet been done" (288) and "about the best description of America that has ever been done" (287), it chronicled the exploits of young Merton Gill who leaves his mundane life as a dry-goods clerk in Simsbury Illinois, moves to Hollywood, and becomes a star despite—and in fact because of—a lack of talent that is equaled only by his good-heartedness and his naïveté. By the early 1920's, an estimated 200,000 aspiring actors came and went in Hollywood *each year* in search of stardom (Leutrat 21), many of them coming from small towns where they had had little or no acting experience but where the now-long-familiar myths of sudden discovery and virtually instant stardom were disseminated in a popular-culture industry that flourished not only in the daily press but also, especially, in the then-new medium of the fan magazine. Even more of a siren song than the familiar "Lullaby of Broadway," the allure of the movies and their proffered ability to transform lives almost overnight afforded a means of escape (in actuality or only in fantasy) that had been unavailable even a generation before—for the characters in James Joyce's *Dubliners* (1904), for example. Yet for every Merton Gill who made the journey westward in search of stardom, hundreds of other men and women remained at home amid mundane cares of the workaday world, against which they nevertheless were nurtured by the fantasy and sustained by the dream. One of these is the subject of Woody Allen's *The Purple Rose of Cairo* (1985), an affectionate and eloquent tribute to the allure and the mystique of the movies. Like Luigi Pirandello's *Six Characters in Search of an Author* (1922), it posits an active interchange between "characters" and "real people": a movie character steps off the screen into the life of an ardent moviegoer, who later temporarily crosses over into his on-screen world as well. Yet whereas Pirandello's work concerns the interaction of actors and characters in establishing the "real" in the theater (the characters interrupt a play rehearsal), *The Purple Rose of Cairo* is uniquely metacinematic, in that it contains a black-and-white 1930s style romance of the same name; its romantic fantasy between a movie character and a moviegoer is thus a counterpart to the on-screen romance that is an affectionate parody of movies of the 1920s and 1930s. Allen's plot incorporates not only the relationship between characters, actors, and "real life," much as Pirandello's play did, but it also emphasizes the unique role and nature of film as a cultural commodity. Its humor therefore extends well beyond the scope of Pirandello's metatheater, so that it encompasses the role of the audience, the producers and distributors, the theater management, and even the nature of cinema itself as a projection of light as well as a projection of its audience's hopes, fantasies, and dreams.

Notwithstanding the originality of the comedy in *The Purple Rose of Cairo*, there are significant precedents for it both within Allen's own writings and in film history. The best-known example, of course, is the use of Humphrey Bogart as a counselor for Allen Felix in the play *Play It Again, Sam* (1969); in the film version (1972), scenes from *Casablanca* are intercut with the present-day action, and the interplay between movies and less-than-heroic everyday life is wittily explored. A more intricate and more relevant parallel, however, is to be found in the short story "The Kugelmass Episode," which was originally published in *The New Yorker* in 1977 and was included in *Side Effects* (1980). There, the title character, a middle-aged professor of English at City College of New York, magically enters the life of Emma Bovary and has an affair with her, brings her temporarily into "real life" of the late 1970s, and appears himself as a character in the texts of the novel that his students read. Yet, the worlds of art and life contaminate each other: Emma, brought into the twentieth century, wants to shop at Bloomingdale's, study acting, win an Oscar, and learn more about O.J. Simpson (an uncannily prescient joke); she is, note, "film-struck." Kugelmass, seeking in literature a romance that he cannot find in real life (exactly as Emma herself did), finds fantasized bliss unsustainable. However, the story does not end in suicide as Flaubert's did; instead, Kugelmass is stranded in a book of *Remedial Spanish*, pursued forever by a Pac-Man-like, voraciously hungry irregular verb. The movies provide an even more alluring world for such fantasies in *The Purple Rose of Cairo*, offering an alternate reality that is simultaneously "there" and "not there" as it is projected on the screen, not bound in words alone. That premise had been explored in Buster Keaton's *Sherlock Jr.* (1924), in which a film projectionist enters the onscreen realm, where he is disconcerted by film's discontinuities, finding that he is unable to adapt quickly enough as scenes are cut from one to the next. The "real" are thus ill equipped to deal with the exigencies of film life, and in one instance one of the characters throws him from the screen and back into his "real world." Screen life is thus also fundamentally unlike stage life as well, where an interloper from the audience could, however disruptively, remain. As Walter Kerr has remarked in *The Silent Clowns*,

> The stage . . . is a medium which explores life on life's terms. Film explores life on film's terms, which is quite a different, indeed a devastatingly different, matter. It may do some of the things other forms do. But it does then uniquely, requires unique forms of perception, has untranslatable habits. (229)

This fact fundamentally separates *The Purple Rose of Cairo* from both "The Kugelmass Episode" and Pirandello's *Six Characters in Search of an Author*. Allen insists, however, that *Sherlock Jr.* "was in no remote way an inspiration" for his film (Björkman, 148).

The selection of the 1930s for the setting of *The Purple Rose of Cairo* emphasizes the difference between the real world of the Great Depression and the black-and-white, on-screen world of elegance and "madcap" adventure. Amid the drab colors of actual life (production design by Stuart Wurtzel, costume design by Jeffrey Kurland, director of photography Gordon Willis), the bright and colorful lights of the marquee of The Jewel movie theater gleam in the twilight; beacon-like, it offers refuge and an escape for the price of a ticket. Cecelia (Mia Farrow), a waitress in a local diner somewhere in New Jersey, is one of the Jewel's most regular customers—the only one in the film who greets the theater's staff by name and is known by name by them. In contrast to her sister (Stephanie Farrow), who is also a waitress at the diner, Cecelia has an extensive and sure knowledge of the movies' plots as well as of their stars' lives; when she talks of Hollywood, her voice is steady, rapid and confident, though she is timid, hesitant and apologetic the rest of the time. Her fascination with the movies distracts her from effectively doing her job: she drops plates, mixes up orders, is late with checks, and repeatedly has to apologize to her customers and to her boss. Her husband Monk (Danny Aiello) has long been unemployed and, with his buddies, passes time pitching pennies outside a closed factory's walls; he cadges money from her tips, demands his dinner when she arrives home, hits her "when [she] get[s] out of line" (342), and secretly dallies with another woman while Cecelia is at the movies. Inside the Jewel, however, Cecelia gazes in rapt attention at a world of elegance and adventure, as unattainable as it is alluring, an unfulfillable desire. The words to Irving Berlin's "Cheek to Cheek," sung by Fred Astaire during the opening credits of Allen's film, aptly describe the movie-going experience itself: while at the movies, Cecelia is indeed in a kind of heaven, "seem[ing] to find the happiness [she] seek[s]" in, quite literally, a better world than this.

The film that Cecelia watches—and of which the audience of Allen's film sees selected black-and-white scenes, sometimes framed by the color proscenium around the movie screen—is an example of what he has described as "one of those films I saw as a kid, what I called 'champagne comedies'—those comedies from the 1930s and 1940s with all those romantic people who wore tuxedos and went to big nightclubs and lived in penthouses and drank champagne all the time" (Björkman, 149). In fact, such films had been popular since the mid-1920s, to whose zeitgeist the "madcap weekend"of frivolity and affluence, whether in New York City night clubs or elegant houses, was far more germane. They were parodied in the Marx Brothers' *Animal Crackers* (1930, dir. Victor Heerman; earlier a hit on the stage), in which Groucho plays Captain Spaulding—an "African explorer" like Tom Baxter in *Purple Rose*—who happens in on the elegant house party of Mrs. Rittenhouse (the ever-staid Margaret Dumont, much like The Countess played by Zoe Caldwell in *Purple Rose*). Henry Adams, the lead character in *Purple Rose*, is a dapper and debonair playwright and playboy who, on impulse, proposes a few weeks in "Morocco or Egypt" with "maybe a stop in Casablanca or Tangiers" before returning "in time for the opening of my new play" (330–331); Jason, his manservant, serves champagne from the art deco bar of the Manhattan penthouse and is ever ready to cable for the "usual suite at the Ritz" in Paris; Rita, Henry's current girlfriend, a Jean Harlow-esque blonde heiress, assures him she has "just the dress to wear to the Pyramids" (331), where, in the next scene they meet Tom Baxter, self-styled "explorer, adventurer . . . doing a little archaeological work"

(333) from which nevertheless he can be distracted at least long enough to join them for a weekend in New York. There, a fortune teller has told him, he will fall in love—as, surely, any member of the movie's audience could have predicted too. Yet, notwithstanding the implausibility of its plot, the clichés of its dialogue, and the fatuity of its characters, *The Purple Rose of Cairo* holds its audience quite literally entranced; Cecilia, like the other moviegoers with her, is shown "totally absorbed" (331) and "eating her popcorn almost automatically . . . mesmerized by the screen " (334) and its glimpse of a world that could not be more unlike her own— which is, of course, a key part of its appeal. The difference is emphasized even in the opening sequence of the film, as drably clad Cecilia gazes at the movie poster's stylish woman in a "long slinky dress" (321)—a succinct embodiment of all the desire that advertising can generate, the allure, fantasy, and commodification on which the movies (and popular culture in general) thrive.

That allure and fantasy become suddenly real when, during Cecelia's fifth viewing of the movie, explorer-adventurer Tom Baxter (Jeff Daniels) suddenly pauses during one of his lines, addresses Cecelia directly, and steps through the screen, metamorphosing from black-and-white to color and causing one of the women in the audience to faint. Though the other characters try to call him back, noting that "we're in the middle of a story," Tom "want[s] to have a look around" in the real world and declares himself free "after two thousand performances of the same monotonous routine" (352-353); he exits the theater hand in hand with Cecelia, showing an impetuosity and madcap adventurousness that far exceed any that he had been given in the script. Although he is a ideally romantic alternative to both Monk and the bow-tie-wearing exterminator to whom her sister has introduced her in the diner, Tom has only a character's knowledge of the world, which gives him a genial naïveté and innocent charm that are, nonetheless, ill suited to the ways of the world: he has only stage money with which to pay the bill in an expensive restaurant to which he takes Cecelia (384), has never had to bother about details like how to use ignition keys in a getaway car (385), and has no idea what happens in making love to a woman *after* the fade-out of a romantically intense scene (387–388). Whereas that knowledge is eventually explained in a visit to a whorehouse, Tom's love for Cecelia and his innocent faith that "where I come from, people, they don't disappoint. They're consistent. They're reliable" (379) is harder to dislodge. "Y-you don't find that kind in real life," Cecelia replies (379).

While the sentimental romance of Tom and Cecelia unfolds in the "real world," acrimony breaks out both on screen and in the theater itself as the characters, unable to continue the story of the film, wait impatiently for Tom to return and interact with members of the startled audience. Much of the humor here derives from Allen's conception of the characters' existence—in part as if they were in live theater, in part as if they are on film. As if in an individual performance on the live stage, they react to a purely localized event: Tom has left the screen only in the one theater, in one locale, with one "real person," Cecelia; other showings of *The Purple Rose of Cairo* proceed, presumably unaffected, elsewhere. As in live theater, too, the screen characters are aware of the physical presence of their audience: Tom knows, for example, how often Cecelia has attended the movie, and he admits having watched her out of the corner of his eye during some of his scenes; he even acknowledges that he finds it distracting when moviegoers occasionally rattle their popcorn bags (361). Staring straight through the screen as if they were violating the live theater's traditionally invisible "fourth wall," the film's characters can see, hear, and talk with members of the audience as well as the theater's manager and staff. The Countess, especially, speaks with a coarseness unbecoming her ostensible social standing, as she tells an elderly man in the audience "I'm a genuine Countess with a lot of dough, and if that's your wife, she's a tub of guts" (368). Nevertheless, the screen *is* present for them as a literally tangible reality: Rita's cheek flattens as she presses her face against it "as if against glass" (353), and Henry admits that he has no idea how Tom "did it" and "can't get out" of the on-screen world himself (355); the characters are also aware of what reel of the film they are currently in (355) and of the reels in which their own and other characters' entrances are due (359). Furthermore, they are aware of themselves as *projected* beings, imploring the theater manager not to turn off the projector—an action that consigns them to a sort of existential void: "it gets black and we disappear," Henry complains, adding that the theater manager does not "understand what it's like to disappear and be to be nothing . . . to be annihilated" (358–359). He is unconsoled by the age-old bromide of the on-screen priest, Father Donnelly, who advises him to "Take it easy. Easy, my son. We're all in this together": polite meaningless words. There is also a more practical reason for not stopping the projector, as a reporter outside the theater remarks: "if he turns off the projector, [he's] liable to strand this Tom Baxter out in the world someplace" (373), without a movie world to which he can return if he so desires. For reasons both physical and metaphysical, therefore, the projection—if not the show—must go on.

Compelled to "go on" existing but unable to get on with their story, and having occasionally glimpsed the dreaded existential void of nonbe-

ing, the characters must pass their time waiting for an unforeseeable arrival (Tom's return) that may, unknowably, never occur. Fundamentally,
then, they are all counterparts of Vladimir and Estragon in Samuel Beckett's *Waiting for Godot*: unable to depart, unable to affect the outcome of
events that directly control their plight, and unable to know what to do in
the interim, they while away their time and distract themselves from
seemingly inevitable boredom in a variety of predictable if ultimately in-
effectual ways. Father Donnelly reads the Bible (365); Henry and Jason
(master and servant, like Pozzo and Lucky) quarrel between themselves
(355–358); Rita whines that, as an heiress, she does not "have to put up
with" such a plight (355); the Countess complains indignantly that it interferes with her plans (365–367); Delilah the maid takes a drink and
flops onto the couch, suspecting that she is somehow being hustled
(359); eventually the priest breaks out a deck of cards and the men play
pinochle (371). Despite Rita's insistence that, as characters, "we're not
human" (375), they have not only remarkably healthy egos but also differing points of view on the literary themes of the story in which they appear. Jason the manservant is convinced that "this is basically my story . .
. the story of a complex, tortured soul," though Henry of course disagrees, contending that "it's the story of a man's quest for self-fulfill-
ment," namely his own (356); to Rita, "it's the story of the effect of
money on true romance" (357), though the men insist that money has
nothing to do with it. Even Tom Baxter is troubled when Cecelia remarks
that he "isn't the main character" (363) as they chat in an abandoned
amusement park. The on-screen characters' argument, meanwhile, de-
generates into increasingly acrimonious personal attacks, as among their
counterparts in Pirandello's *Six Characters in Search of an Author*. Their
penthouse movie set, however, is a stylishly furnished counterpart of the
stark, almost bare, unescapable interior of Beckett's *Endgame*, from the
windows of which the characters have a very limited view of the world
outside—whose inhabitants, as the Countess remarks of the "real world"
audience of the 1930s, "don't look like they're having too much fun"
(366).

The reaction of the on-screen moviegoers is exactly that of so many
in the first live theater audiences for *Waiting for Godot* or *Six Characters
in Search of an Author*: a progression from bemusement to shock to
moral and/or political outrage to indignant allegations that it is all a
hoax; eventually, inevitably, it culminates in that ultimate cry of the
philistine, "I want my money back" (367, 372, 375, plural 371). A
woman complains that "They just sit around and talk? No action? . . .
Nothing happens?" (367); an angry man exiting the theater says that he

does not "pay to watch those socialites sitting around up there and staring back at us, making nasty remarks" (371); when still another complains that "there's no story" (372), a reporter speculates that "this could
be the work of Reds or anarchists" (372)—perhaps under the pernicious
influence of Anton Chekhov or Luigi Pirandello, it would seem. The latter's theories of time and flux are evoked, albeit quite unknowingly, in
the most metaphysical of the comments from the disgruntled theatergo-
ers: "I want what happened in the movie last week to happen this week, .
. . otherwise what's life all about anyway?" (373). Nevertheless, this new
plotless, talky, and wholly unconventional drama *does* find an audience
of its own, primarily among the curious and those who "don't mind observing"; although that characterization sounds merely voyeuristic, these
moviegoers are self-styled "student[s] of human personality," intrigued
presumably by Chekhovian "interior action"—even if they have "trouble
with live humans" around them (374-375). The theater manager, of
course, willingly sells tickets to all comers, but he concedes to the studio
bosses that "the theater is nine-tenths empty" (376).

Because a movie is physical property in a way that a live theater production is not, corporate management and their lawyers become duly
concerned; there are, at least potentially, "hundreds of Tom Baxters on
the loose" (377), some of them perhaps with criminal intent—a possibility that Pirandello's *Six Characters* could not incorporate. The comic
possibilities for mayhem—and the metaphysical implications that Pirandello raises—are thus compounded exponentially by the unique nature
of film itself. These problems are particularly acute for actor Gil Shepherd (also played by Jeff Daniels) who "created" the Tom Baxter character on screen and, of course, whose exact likeness and voice the runaway
character bears. Now hoping to play Charles Lindbergh in a biographical
feature, Shepherd learns of Tom Baxter's "escape" as he gives a vapid interview to a reporter at a dinner party, quoting positive reviews about
himself but needing to rely on his dialogue coach for answers that re-
quire even minimal thought—and for advice on "work[ing] so hard to
make [Tom] real" in his performance (382). He flies off to New Jersey to
confront and help recapture the character he created, now clearly running
out of control. On the surface level, the film now affords an ironic variation on the Pirandellian conflict between actors and characters, who, in
film as not in the theater, necessarily look exactly alike. More deeply
imbedded, however, is a comic rendition of the myth of Frankenstein—
though the miscreant "escaped creature" here is not a grotesque monster
but the actor's own double, a romantically suave character who is, at
least potentially, reduplicative hundreds of times.

Tom's clandestine liaison with Cecelia thrives, in large part, due to his mastery of romantic rhetoric—"movie talk," as she calls it (387), though she acknowledges that he is a perfect kisser and he embraces her with a tenderness that Monk presumably has never shown. She has lied to Monk, telling him she has a job babysitting, in order to be with Tom, who, nevertheless, remains not only impractical but unreal: he suggests, for example, that they escape to the desert and live on love; in the real world, however, he has neither money nor a job. When film producer Raoul Hirsch and actor Gil Shepherd arrive at the theater, they discover that in the confusion no one noticed the identity of the woman who left with Tom. Gil discovers her through coincidence at a drugstore, where she mistakes him for Tom—a uniquely cinematic variation on the age-old "twin" comedy devices from Plautus to Shakespeare. Cecelia, star-struck and fanzine-addicted, knows all of Gil's movies and reluctantly agrees to take him to Tom, who, she says, wants to remain free. At the closed amusement park, actor and character meet face to face (and appear together in the same shots, in dialogue with each other); they have a brief Pirandellian contretemps over whether the actor or the character makes the role a success (403); Tom declares his love for Cecelia, who admits she finds him perfect, but Gil, protesting that Tom is fictional, asks "What good is 'perfect' if the man's not real?!" (404). Though Tom protests that he can "learn to be real" and insists that "being real comes very naturally to me," Gil threatens to bring in the police, the producers, the Actors Union, and the F.B.I. (404–405). However, as Hirsch points out in the following scene, there has been no crime.

While Cecelia tries to explain to Tom about God (whom the character mistakes for the movie's writers), Monk finds them together, having been tipped off by penny-pitching buddies that she had been out with the pith-helmeted man at the restaurant the night before. Though Tom has had courage "written into [his] character" (410), Monk wins the ensuing fistfight with a low blow; Cecelia refuses to go home with him, however, standing up to her husband for the first time, inspired by Tom's valor. While Cecelia rejoins Gil, who takes her to lunch and is enthralled by her compliments about his career, Tom meets a prostitute at the amusement park and visits her brothel, where he remains preoccupied with metaphysical questions many of which are recurrent preoccupations in Allen's writings. As the (quite sentimentalized) whores query him about his sexual interests (few specifics of which were written into his character), he muses on the existence of God, the finality of death, the miracle of birth, and most importantly "how magical it seems . . . in the real world as, uh, opposed to the world of . . . celluloid and flickering shadows" (424). The latter is also the world of the legendary and elusive "purple rose" of the title, which he is seeking in Egypt when he is introduced in the film. It is in many ways the counterpart of the "green rose" about which Stephen Dedalus fantasizes in Joyce's *Portrait of the Artist as a Young Man*: "you could not have a green rose," he realizes, "but perhaps somewhere in the world you could" (12). That somewhere is, in Joyce's novel and in Allen's film, the world of art, the world of the imagination—and now (unlike in Stephen's day) the world of the movie.

Resolving that "I don't want to talk any more about what's real and what's illusion" and claiming that "life's too short to spend time thinking about life" (440), Tom returns with Cecelia to the theater, introduces her to fellow cast members as his fiancée, and takes her with him into the black-and-white, on-screen world—a sequence that was, Allen has explained in an interview, "a much later afterthought" after he had written the original story (Björkman 148). Like Alice through the looking glass, like Dorothy in the land of Oz, Cecelia in the screen world soon finds that different rules prevail there and things are seldom what they seem. The plot of the on-screen *Purple Rose* resumes at last, with Cecelia becoming an extra character at the party at the Copacabana (like Kugelmass appearing in the pages of *Madame Bovary*), where Tom's stage money is spendable but the on-screen champagne that it buys turns out to be merely ginger ale. Cecelia's presence in the "reel world" is almost as disruptive as Tom's presence in "real life"; she is an unexpected rival to the nightclub singer Kitty Haynes, whom he is scripted to marry in every show. "Chucking out the plot," Tom declares "it's every man for himself!" and takes Cecelia on a tour of Manhattan's most famous nightclubs (449). During a romantic scene in the penthouse, Gil interrupts by walking into the movie theater; he becomes jealous, and brings them back through the screen yet again to reality. Both suitors proclaim their love for her, and she must choose; though she protests that she is already married, Gil tempts her to run away with him to Hollywood. Her decision is inevitable, simply but eloquently expressed to Tom:

> See, I'm a real person. No matter how . . . how tempted I am I have to choose the real world. (459)

Having so chosen, she returns to her apartment and begins to pack, defying the stunned Monk who, as he had done on her previous attempt to leave him (when she discovered his adultery), assures her that she will

"See what it is out there! It ain't the movies! It's real life! It's real life, and you'll be back!" (464). Carrying her suitcase and the ukelele that Gil had asked her to bring (having shared a song with her in a typical 1920s or 1930s style musical vignette several scenes earlier), she goes to the theater to meet Gil, escape to Hollywood, and fulfill her dreams. Her hopes are dashed by the reality that Gil has already left for Hollywood, having gotten Tom Baxter safely back on the screen. *The Purple Rose of Cairo* has left town, replaced by the musical *Top Hat* with Fred Astaire and Ginger Rogers, which Cecelia buys a ticket to see. In the final sequence of the film, Cecelia is again in the audience at the Jewel, engrossed in the latest movie, yearning and sad but no longer crying. After a particularly spectacular dance sequence that is intercut with the shots of her sitting in the audience, she begins to smile, transported out of herself and away from her workaday cares yet again by the movies.

Like the characters in Joyce's *Dubliners*, Cecelia suffers from a kind of spiritual paralysis that makes her escape impossible and the bittersweet ending of *The Purple Rose of Cairo* so appropriate; it is, in fact, the inevitable ending that any such film would have had in the 1930s, when, under the Hays Code of censorship, infidelity was never to be rewarded and marriage was ever to be affirmed. Along with *Broadway Danny Rose* (1984) and *Radio Days* (1987), *The Purple Rose of Cairo* celebrates the popular culture of a now-gone era whose innocence gives it a particular charm that the neurosis-wracked characters of Allen's more contemporary (and more characteristic) comedies necessarily lack. Like *Zelig* (1983), it displays his particular delight in the unique capabilities of film as a medium. *Purple Rose*, he contends, "has always been a favorite [among his films], because I had an idea, and I got the idea on the screen as I wanted it" (Björkman 81). But beyond its technical virtuosity, its clever plotting, its metacinematic dazzlement and its provocative metaphysical implications, its seemingly uncomplicated character Cecelia, raptly gazing at the movie screen, may well prove to be one of the most enduring images from all of Woody Allen's films. She is, in many ways, the complement to and counterpart of Merton Gill—an American classic, extraordinary in part because she is so ordinary, the moviegoer in us all.

Bibliography

Allen, Woody. *Play It Again, Sam* [film version]. Ed. Richard Anobile. New York: Grosset and Dunlap, 1977.

——. *Play It Again, Sam* [stage version]. New York: Samuel French, 1969.

——. "The Purple Rose of Cairo." In *Three Films of Woody Allen.* 317–473 New York: Random House, 1987.

——. "The Kugelmass Episode." In *Side Effects*. 41–55 New York: Random House, 1980.

Beckett, Samuel. *Endgame*. New York: Grove Press, 1958.

——. *Waiting for Godot*. New York: Grove Press, 1954.

Björkman, Stig. *Woody Allen on Woody Allen: In Conversation with Stig Björkman*. New York: Grove Press, 1993.

Joyce, James. *Dubliners*. Ed. John Wyse Jackson and Bernard McGinley. New York: St. Martin's Press, 1993.

——. *A Portrait of the Artist as a Young Man*. Ed. Richard Ellmann. New York: Viking, 1964.

Kerr, Walter. *The Silent Clowns*. New York: Knopf, 1979.

Lax, Eric. *Woody Allen: A Biography*. New York: Knopf, 1991.

Leutrat, Jean-Louis. "Merton Gill, un homme ordinarie du cinéma des années 1920." *Revue française d'études américaines* 19.9 (February 1984): 19–31.

Pirandello, Luigi. *Six Characters in Search of an Author*. Trans. Edward Storer. 1387-1432 *The Norton Anthology of World Masterpieces*. Ed. Maynard Mack et al. 5th ed. Vol. 2.

Stein, Gertrude. *Everybody's Autobiography*. New York: Random House, 1937.

Wilson, Harry Leon. *Merton of the Movies*. New York: Doubleday, Page & Co.

Yacowar, Maurice. *Loser Take All: The Comic Art of Woody Allen*. New expanded edition. New York: Continuum, 1991.

Woody's Alice and Alan's Susan
A Tale of Two Women

KAREN C. BLANSFIELD

At first glance, Woody Allen and Alan Ayckbourn don't seem likely literary bedfellows, though both are notably prolific and popular, both explore marriage and relationships, and both have charted recognizable
social territory—Allen the world of prosperous New Yorkers, Ayckbourn
that of middle-class Englishmen. Still, Allen's 1990 film *Alice* bears interesting comparison to Ayckbourn's 1985 play *Woman in Mind*, which
many critics regarded as a turning point in that playwright's work.
Allen's film and Ayckbourn's play both focus on a central female character who is unhappy in her marriage and dissatisfied with her life; more
importantly, both are highly imaginative in style, exploring their subjects
through elements of fantasy, magic, and hallucination, with touches of
the supernatural. But while *Alice* is whimsical and entertaining, offering
a positive and even uplifting outcome, *Woman in Mind* is darker and
more bleak, presenting a descent into madness that, while certainly humorous, is in the end decidedly dismal.

The title characters are both women near middle age, long married
and settled into their lives, both with children and husbands to whom
they are accustomed, if not comfortable. Alice Tate (Mia Farrow) be-
longs to Allen's typical affluent milieu of Manhattan's Upper East Side.
The trophy wife of a wealthy Wall Street stockbroker named Doug
(William Hurt), Alice lives a leisured but lackluster life of luncheons,
beauty parlor appointments, and socializing, complete with nanny and
personal buyer. As she says, "I've become one of those women who
shops all day and has pedicures." Susan Gannet, by contrast, is "an unas-
suming woman in her forties, used to and happy to play second fiddle to

more determined personalities than her own," but who, after many years, is "beginning to question this role she's played or perhaps been cast in" (*Woman in Mind* 9).¹ Though *Woman in Mind* doesn't forefront class distinctions as overtly as other Ayckbourn plays, Susan clearly belongs to a dull, middle-class world. Her husband Gerald is a smug, provincial vicar, with an eccentric, shrewish sister who augments the gloom, while Susan and Gerald's son Rick is distant and uncommunicative. Not surprisingly, the imaginary family Susan dreams up to offset this dreary trio is distinctly different. Wealthy, refined, and leisurely, the group features a loving husband, a handsome brother, and an adoring daughter, with Susan herself transformed into an important individual, though with changing identities—first she's a leading historical novelist, then a major heart surgeon. Moreover, this family lives a life more akin to Alice's: playing tennis, drinking champagne at noon, and dwelling on an immense estate complete with lake, expansive lawn, herb garden, and rose beds. Upward mobility is part of Susan's fantasy, whereas Alice seeks escape from its superficiality and emptiness.

Allen and Ayckbourn are quite inventive and daring in exploring their heroines' situations, though Allen uses an assortment of experiments while Ayckbourn is singular and consistent, developing the play primarily through the central character's viewpoint. Alice, in keeping with her namesake, steps through a kind of looking glass with the aid of magical herbs and potions supplied by the mysterious Dr. Yang. She becomes invisible, travels through time, converses with the dead, and flies through the night skies. Susan enjoys no such merriment; the novelty in Ayckbourn's play is a visual perspective equivalent to that of a first-person narrator. "Throughout the play," notes Ayckbourn in the opening stage directions, "we will hear what she hears; see what she sees. A subjective viewpoint therefore and one that may at times be somewhat less than accurate" (9). Thus, for instance, the play begins in a "small, tidy, suburban garden" (9), but as Susan moves into her fantasy world, "it grows imperceptibly bigger and lighter" (12). Toward the end Susan's insanity intensifies, and *"Everything from here on is in a slightly heightened colour and design, suggesting SUSAN's own extreme mental state"*; the images subsequently seen are her memories of films, books, and television (82).

Interestingly, Allen's film is sometimes theatrical, while Ayckbourn's play is filmic in its subjective perspective. Allen, for example, uses circus-style spotlights, as when Alice's dead boyfriend Eddie vanishes, leaving only an empty circle of light. In another scene, Alice converses with her mother (Gwen Verdon) on a theater stage against the glare of lights; Alice tells her mother that she was wrong to forego a design career in favor of marrying Doug, revealing that, in a sense, she has been performing all her life. In *Woman in Mind*, Susan's skewed perspective is similar to the view a camera lens might convey. The Scarborough production emphasized this subjective angle, with the real and fantasy families occupying the same stage space, though with different lighting and costumes. "The result," notes Bernard Dukore, "was so subtle a demonstration of her ideal world impinging on the actual world that until well into the first act one was uncertain whether her imaginary family were actually real" (77). Ayckbourn himself said of this rather daring experiment, "I wanted to write a first person narrative, a play seen, like a film, through the lens of a hand held camera. A play that would do the very thing one is careful to avoid as a dramatist. That is, break the rules, undermine the normal logic, slowly rob the situation of reality" (Holt 43–44).

Both *Alice* and *Woman in Mind* begin to some degree in fantasy, with the audience unaware of the illusion and thus easily drawn in.[2] *Alice* opens against the backdrop of the penguin exhibit at Central Park Zoo, with the title character passionately kissing a man whom we later learn to be Joe Ruffolo (Joe Mantegna), a suitably virile saxophone player on a slightly lower social rung than Alice. No words are exchanged, and a moment later, the scene shifts to Alice daydreaming in her kitchen as her husband asks, "Hey, where are you now?" He then goes on to discuss the proper seating arrangements for that night's dinner party. The first few moments of *Woman in Mind* are more psychological and also more baffling. Susan, lying on the grass and emerging from unconsciousness, engages in what seems to be nonsensical dialogue with Dr. Bill Windsor, as the first few lines illustrate:

> BILL. Ah! Score ache . . .
> SUSAN. (*Trying to sit up*) Waah . . .
> BILL. Wo! Won't spider slit up pikelet . . .
> SUSAN. What?
> BILL. Skater baby.
> SUSAN. (*Trying again to sit up, alarmed*) What are you saying
> — (*Clasping her head*) — Ah!
> BILL. (*Pushing her back, gently*) Squeezy . . . squeezy . . .
> SUSAN. Squeezy?

As Susan's perception clears, so does the dialogue, which has been blurred by her semi-conscious state. A few minutes later, when she seems to be all right and the doctor leaves to fetch her a cup of tea, Susan's husband, brother, and daughter come onto the scene. Naturally, the audience assumes they are real people, only to discover—after her real family enters—that they exist only in Susan's mind. As Michael Holt notes, "Susan and the audience are in the same situation. They are both aware that reality has been disturbed and perception upset . . . [and] they are not very clear with which set of characters to engage" (42). As with *Alice*, viewers have been tricked, lured unknowingly into a fantasy world, only to be startled back to reality—twice, in Ayckbourn's scenario. In both cases, the effect is an immediate engagement with the main character, giving both Alice and Susan the edge in gaining audience sympathy, or at least empathy. Both times we begin in the character's head so that we see the world from their viewpoints, thus setting the expectation for internal and external realities, which will eventually merge to differing extents—Alice being able to distinguish between the two while Susan is not.

Furthermore, at the outset of both film and play, the two women are afflicted by some kind of physical ailment, one that proves to be intrinsically connected to an emotional one. Alice complains of a backache that neither her masseuse, chiropractor, nor personal trainer has been able to cure, and when she seeks medical attention, she is told that the problem is really in her mind. "Problem is not in back," advises Dr. Yang. "Problem is here, here," pointing first to his head, then his heart. "Nothing wrong with back." Susan, on the other hand, has suffered a concussion from the farcical action of stepping on a garden rake, and a doctor is present as she regains consciousness. Her injury, unlike Alice's, is indeed real, but it triggers a deep-seated psychological malady, resulting in a delirium that ultimately engulfs her.[3] Though the implication in the play is that Susan's hallucinations result from her injury, the familiarity of these imaginary characters suggests also that she could have experienced these delusions before, and the fact that she has long been unhappy reinforces this interpretation.

Alice's visits to Dr. Yang and his mystical treatments help her define and address her discontent. When she first goes to his office in Chinatown (arriving conspicuously in a black stretch limousine), Dr. Yang hypnotizes her and asks what she sees; her response indicates her suppressed confusion: "Penguins—they mate for life," Alice replies. "The man—he kisses me. I want to know him better. My feelings are too scary. Feelings for my husband are different . . . I love him, but I . . . ," and she trails off. When Dr. Yang then tells Alice that Doug is in the room, she articulates her feelings directly to him: "I'm the wife. I take care of the kids, I host the dinner parties, arrange the social schedule, try to look pretty so your friends can admire your taste. . . . But I'm—I want to be more. There's more to me. . . . I want to do something with my life before it's too late. . . . I gave up a career to marry you."

By contrast, Susan seems to have long been aware of the reasons for her boredom and unhappiness. That she is alienated from her physical environment is clear from her response to Bill when he tries to correct her deluded perception of her "estate"; she says he's "describing some place I wouldn't choose to live in, even in my wildest nightmares" (21). Like Alice, Susan further articulates her unhappiness to her husband: "I used to be a wife. I used to be a mother. And I loved it. People said, Oh, don't you long to get out and do a proper job? And I'd say, No thanks, this is a proper job, thank you. Mind your own business. But now it isn't any more. The thrill has gone" (24). Like Alice, Susan finds that the role "she's played or perhaps been cast in" no longer satisfies her, though she doesn't directly blame her husband (9). "It's nobody's fault," she tells Gerald. "It just happened, over the years" (27).

Nevertheless, both Alice and Susan have been emotionally and/or physically neglected by their husbands. Alice's marriage is one of ap-pearances, as befits her status-conscious, ladder-climbing husband, whose idea of a conflict is whether to buy a Lincoln or a Cadillac (though he really wants a Bentley). Doug dismisses Alice's attempts to discuss her needs, her desire to work, and her interest in writing, suggesting that he can set her up in a sweater boutique a friend of his is bankrolling for his equally bored wife. Still, Alice—like Susan—is reluctant to blame her husband for her condition; as she says, "I'm at a crossroads. I'm lost." Only later does she learn that Doug has been cheating on her for years, and through a magic potion that makes her invisible, she catches him red-handed at an office Christmas party.

Susan, too, seems peripheral to her husband, whom she no longer loves, nor he her. "We don't kiss," Susan tells Gerald. "We hardly touch each other—we don't make love—we don't even share the same bed now. We sleep at different ends of the room" (26). Like Doug, Gerald is preoccupied with his work—in his case, writing a book about his parish history—and is indifferent to his wife's suffering. When she says she isn't happy, he replies, "Well, who is? These days. Very few" (23). He claims she needs to keep busier and spouts platitudes like, " 'The trivial round, the common task,/Will furnish all we need to ask . . .' " (24). It's ironic, then, that Gerald is a minister, not only because of his insensitivity—a common characteristic of Ayckbourn's men—but also because, though he claims himself to be "a specialist in matters unseen," he puts no stock in and shows no concern for Susan's hallucinations (25).

Religion, in fact, permeates both *Alice* and *Woman in Mind*. Alice, like so many of Allen's neurotic, spiritually barren characters, struggles with guilt and seeks salvation from her emotional and spiritual angst. Her strong Catholic upbringing defines her beliefs and actions and "will be very important to her in the creation of her new identity" (Lee 292). Alice's firm belief in fidelity accounts for her distress over her attraction to Joe, and her comments throughout the film—as well as her ultimate rejection of materialism—attest to her strong faith and her spiritual needs. She tells her sister how she loved the mass and the rituals; she jokingly says to Joe, "There's nothing sexier than a lapsed Catholic"; she's concerned that she isn't raising her children with the right values; and when she gets to eavesdrop on her gossipy friends because she's invisible, she says, "I'll definitely go straight to hell." But perhaps the most revealing moment in the film comes when Alice returns to the house where she grew up, which is filled with Catholic symbols, including a confessional in the front yard, and recalls her long-ago dreams: "When I was young I wanted to be a saint," she says. "I used to pray with my arms outstretched because it was more painful, and I could feel closer to God. I wanted to spend my life helping people, taking care of the sick, and the old people. I was never happier than when I got a chance to help out that way. What happened? Where did that part of me go?" In the end, her benevolent urges win out: after a stint in Calcutta with Mother Teresa, Alice moves herself and her children to a simple, servant-free apartment and settles into a life of caring for the disadvantaged.

Susan Gannet, though not herself on a spiritual quest, is surrounded by various permutations of religion. Besides her husband the vicar, there is Gerald's sister Muriel, who subscribes to a kind of eccentric spiritualism, "a form of psychic self-delusion," believing that her late husband is trying to communicate with her by writing on the ceiling (Billington 186). Gerald's and Susan's son Rick joins a Moonie-like cult that forbids its members to talk with their parents, a comical vow of silence that is symptomatic of Susan's inability to communicate with anyone in her family. Numerous other references to religious belief delineate the play: when Susan first emerges from unconsciousness, she fears she has "died and gone to hell" (10); Rick recalls his father's apprehension of any woman he dated and his terror that "they'd turn out to be the daughters of Beelzebub" (56); and Gerald, forced to drink his sister's lousy hot chocolate, laments, "[C]ompulsory cocoa. Locusts follow shortly" (81). The two most overt allusions, which come near the end of the play, are Susan's sudden horrified recognition as Andy is kissing her—"Oh, dear God! I'm making love with the Devil . . . "—before surrendering "to the happily inevitable" (76), and the mysterious fire that breaks out in Gerald's study, a clear manifestation of evil. Critic Michael Billington has described *Woman in Mind* as "not only about an emotionally neglected middle-aged woman's descent into madness but also about the failure of orthodox Christian morality to cope with individual unhappiness" (165). In Ayckbourn's view, argues Billington, religion fails to cope with contemporary mental distress, and like Alan Bennett, Ayckbourn regards churchmen as too often indifferent toward the suffering around them (185). Susan, deserted "in her hour of crisis by God's representative and Christian love," falls into the now-Satanic arms of Andy (Billington 186).

To some degree, then, both *Alice* and *Woman in Mind* address the broader social concern of religion and its failure to satisfy and fulfill individual needs. In an interview, Allen said, "Conflict between despair and hope can only be resolved on an individual basis, not in any general theoretical way. Faith can't be come to by reason—it's a gift, perhaps even a blind spot or flaw, but helpful, like [a] denial mechanism" (Lee 374). Similarly, in Ayckbourn's view, no religious approach seems to offer solace: not the vicar's, not Muriel's spiritualist nonsense, not the son's Trappist silence.

In exploring their characters' struggles and dilemmas, both Allen and Ayckbourn delve into the fantastic, though in different ways and to different degrees. In Allen's film, the magical encounters are buoyant and enlightening, while in Ayckbourn's play they are initially frivolous but ultimately dangerous, frightening, and destructive. One key difference between the two works is that Alice recognizes her phantoms; they are people from her past—her mother and her lover, Eddie, who was killed in a car crash, a la James Dean—and they are also consistent throughout the film. In addition, Alice's engagement with these ghosts is positive and beneficial; her conversations with them help her "to gain insights into her own current situation" (Lee 293). Eddie guides Alice in developing her relationship with Joe, advising her to "see this thing through, find out who he is, who you are." Her mother, though not particularly supportive of Alice, does enable her to see that her marriage to Doug was the wrong choice. Furthermore, Alice summons her ghosts, though not always knowingly. She drinks potions, smokes opium, and burns herbs at midnight. Dr. Yang even implies her visions might have a religious dimension. "Mrs. Tate believes in ghosts," he says. "Don't all Catholics? . . . In times of great stress, sometimes ghosts appear."

Susan, on the other hand, has created her phantoms, though they come to be recognizable to her. They are rooted in her own reality, being polar opposites of their counterparts in reality.[4] Initially, they are beneficial to her: they offer a happiness and lightness not available through Gerald, Rick, and Muriel. But unlike Alice's ghosts, Susan's change through the course of the play. In act 2 they become intrusive and bothersome, aborting attempts to communicate with her son Rick, putting words in her mouth, ignoring her commands to leave, and finally turning on her. Tony's arrival with a bloodstained game bag just after the neighbor's dog has disappeared suggests a murderous instinct on his part, and when Bill enters Susan's fantasy world, Andy tells Tony to "chuck him in the lake" but to "[d]o it gently" (*Woman* 75). By the end, as Susan grows increasingly frantic, her fantasy and real families have become fully integrated and are completely ignoring her. She descends deeper into the aphasia that began the play, spouting seeming nonsense in the blue flashing light of an ambulance:

> SUSAN. . . . Hair growing, hens? Goosey? Gandy? Chair old? (*Pause*). Hair shone? Hair hall shone? Tone show, fleas. Fleas, tone show. December bee? Choose 'un. December choosey. December bee? December bee?
> (*The others have frozen in the shadows. They appear neither to see nor to hear her now.*
> SUSAN *gives a last despairing wail. As she does so, the lights fade to blackout*) (*Woman* 91-92).

The very subtitle of the play, *December Bee*, evokes the notion of ghosts. The phrase is Susan's garbled rendition of "remember me," which as Billington points out, is invariably reminiscent of the ghost in *Hamlet* imploring his son to avenge his untimely death. Billington, in fact, sees a strong resemblance between the two plays: "Like *Hamlet*, *Woman in Mind* is a play in which the protagonist is driven into a state of madness and is prey to visitation by equivocal phantoms . . . who may be uttering important truths or who may be evil enchanters," and he argues that Susan's alienation from her surroundings, like Hamlet's, helps to at least partially induce this madness (182–83).

The outcomes of *Alice* and *Woman in Mind* are quite different, not least because one is happy, the other sad. In the end, Alice changes; she becomes more assertive and ultimately takes control of her life, even though, as one critic wryly observes, she "seems to be one of the last women in the Western world to wake up to feminism" (Johnson 50). Alice is eventually "able to see herself and make the decisions that will transform her from a young, sheltered girl into a mature woman who chooses to take full responsibility for her life" (Lee 297). Susan, however, doesn't have the benefit of choice. Where Alice emerges from the looking glass transformed, Susan descends further and finally into madness. Unable to define herself and losing control of her own fantasy, Susan is a woman who succumbs to her "first, shell-shocking encounter with her own despair" (Rich 580).

Allen's *Alice* and Ayckbourn's *Woman in Mind* both delve into the female psyche, one in a comic way, the other in a tragic. Such a foray is not new for either writer, though it is more unusual for Allen, who tends to explore female characters in terms of relationships, while Ayckbourn has developed a reputation as a feminist writer. While both treatments are sympathetic, Susan's inconsistencies raise doubts about her reliability, which in turn may affect one's judgment of her. Her version of raising Rick, for instance, differs sharply from his, and she condemns her husband both for talking too much and talking too little.

Most significantly, perhaps, Allen's film and Ayckbourn's play both raise questions about the relationship between fantasy and reality, the consequences or benefits of confusing the two, and even the nature of the medium itself. Film is inherently illusory, and *Alice* challenges viewers to examine the relationship between reality and fantasy, just as the main character must. Alice's escape into her wonderland is ultimately redemptive, a benefit that moviegoers may also enjoy. Theatre, by contrast, is live, and so the sense of escapism is somewhat tempered. *Woman in Mind*, in appropriating film technique, explores not only the division between illusion and reality but also the fine line between sanity and insanity. As Billington points out, "if the play were simply contrasting reality and fantasy, it would offer a one-way ticket to nowhere: what it actually says is that the inability to distinguish between the two is a clinical symptom of madness" (184). In the end, both women's lives are shaped by their illusions: for Alice, fantasy provides a kind of escape, and a benign one, but for Susan, fantasy turns predatory and ultimately proves fatal. Together, Allen's Alice and Ayckbourn's Susan offer poignant if disturbingly different insights into the power of a woman in mind.

Notes

1. All subsequent references to Ayckbourn's play will be cited simply as *Woman*.

2. When starting production on *Alice*, Allen sent a memo to his crew that read in part, "The film begins with the usual CREDITS and then the OPENING SHOT will be a fantasy, although we won't know it at first" (Lax 321).

3. In exploring the realm of madness, Ayckbourn has acknowledged his debt to Oliver Sacks's remarkable work, *The Man Who Mistook His Wife For A Hat* (Billington 184).

4. Frank Rich compares this play to another Woody Allen film, *The Purple Rose of Cairo*, noting that Susan's imaginary relatives "step into [her] suburban garden much as the glamorous Jeff Daniels stepped out of the movie screen into Mia Farrow's drab life" (580).

Works Cited

Allen, Woody. *Alice*. Orion, 1990.

Ayckbourn, Alan. *Woman in Mind (December Bee)*. London: Faber & Faber, 1986.

Billington, Michael. *Alan Ayckbourn*. New York: St. Martin's Press, 1983, 1990.

Dukore, Bernard, ed. *Alan Ayckbourn: A Casebook*. New York: Garland 1991.

Holt, Michael. *Alan Ayckbourn*. Plymouth: Northcote House, 1999.

Johnson, Brian D. "Alice." *Maclean's*, 28 Jan. 1991: 49–50.

Lax, Eric. *Woody Allen: A Biography*. New York: Vintage Books, 1992.

Lee, Sander H. *Woody Allen's Angst: Philosophical Commentaries on His Serious Films*. London: McFarland & Co., 1997.

Rich, Frank. "Woman in Mind." *Hot Seat: Theater Criticism for The New York Times, 1980-1993*. New York: Random House, 1998: 579–81.

Oh Sweet Diabolical Muse
Creation and Retreat in Woody Allen's *Deconstructing Harry, Celebrity,* and Other Recent Films

GAYLORD BREWER

> Because what the writer does—the filmmaker or the writer—you create a world that you would like to live in. You like the people you create. You like what they wear, where they live, how they talk, and it gives you a chance for some months to live in that world. And those people move to beautiful music, and you're in that world. So in my films I just feel there's always a pervasive feeling of the greatness of idealized life or fantasy versus the unpleasantness of reality.
> —Woody Allen

Woody Allen has often elaborated on his love of writing as the most unadulterated aspect of his career. He told Eric Lax that "I like the pure joy of waking up in my house, having my breakfast, going into a room by myself, and writing. It's pleasurable because it's lazy and escapist. You don't have to deal with anybody, you don't have to see anybody, you're never on the line" (220). Allen's recent films continue to explore his interest in fantasy and reality in the context of the writer at work. Two recent films in particular, *Deconstructing Harry* (1997) and *Celebrity* (1998), are controversial recastings of Allen personae and variations on the costs and consequences of artistic success. In *Deconstructing Harry,* Allen offers his most excoriating study yet on the effects of creation on the artist and his subjects, while in *Celebrity* this theme is reconfigured to focus specifically on the writer who sacrifices literary integrity for a vain dream of entry into the circle of fame.

The connection between Allen's love of the private writing act and the obsessive, confessional habit of his character Harry Block is perhaps inescapable to any discussion of *Deconstructing Harry*. In this incarnation, Allen's writer-protagonist is neither frustrated television writer/comic, failed novelist, nor compromised filmmaker, the most common guises of the recurring type—he is a successful fiction writer. The film grimly depicts the writer as exploiter. Leonard Quart notes that while Harry resembles earlier Allen portrayals in that "he still whines, and is death-obsessed, and at odds with the natural world," Harry is differentiated because "he no longer is that 'superior' being who solemnly moralizes about other people's corrupt behavior." (34). David Ansen calls the film Allen's "bleakest, most self-punishing comedy" (85), while Stanley Kauffmann observes that the figure of Harry is such a "despicable, exploitative, deceptive egotist that an authentic performance of the role . . . would have made him unbearable" ("New York" 24). Certainly, Allen's choice to play Harry himself was daring. The self-effacing mannerisms of the Allen persona serve as a buffer to Harry's otherwise bilious manipulations of those who make the mistake of being involved with him.

Sam B. Girgus argues that "the merging of art and reality, normality and neurosis, has comprised the core" of Allen's films. "The testing of taboos and prohibitions and the craving for impossible love have been pervasive" (ix). In *Manhattan* (1979), Isaac is the writer manqué found so often in the films. When an ex-wife publishes a confessional expose of their failed marriage—"he longed to be an artist but balked at the necessary sacrifices"—Isaac is the wounded and indignant "victim" of literature's cruel prerogative. At the conclusion of *Annie Hall* (1977)—a film that Maurice Yacowar describes as primarily concerned with the "power of art to compensate for the limitations of life" (179)—Alvy's play is a verbatim transcription of his final moments with Annie, but the effect is comic. The character apologizes for his feeble effort to try "to get things to come out perfect in art," a benign attempt at catharsis. The effect of confessional art is also softened in *Hannah and Her Sisters* (1986). While Holly's first script is merciless, her second attempt is softened by humor, then all writing is presumably silenced by marriage and pregnancy.

Perhaps the most direct precursor to Harry Block is the autobiographical novelist Gabe in Allen's caustic *Husbands and Wives* (1992).

"Should I be insulted?" his wife asks, recognizing the "description of the way we met" in Gabe's manuscript. Further, Gabe's attraction to "Kamikaze women," "maybe because [he's] a writer," anticipates Harry Block's later self-analysis. Even in *Husbands and Wives,* however, a harsh reaction to the Allen character is modified in two ways: by his creative frustrations and by the presence of Rain, a prodigy of confessional exploitation. Faced with her rapid recital of recent lovers, Gabe responds, amazed, "God, you've got material for your first novel, and the sequel, and an opera by Puccini here." While both take for granted that personal relationships, not imagination, are the compost of fiction, Rain seems the more dangerous. Her ominous prophecy for their aborted relationship—"I know how it would end"—casually recognizes an inevitable self-preservation. At the film's end, Gabe informs us that his new novel is "less confessional, more political. Can I go? Is this over?" Damaged by relationships, he retreats to attempt a different type of art.

Deconstructing Harry begins with visual discontinuity. Between black-screen credits Lucy, one of Harry's exploited lovers, approaches his door through repeated jump cuts. The film then offers Harry's fictional account of her betrayal before the "real" scene ensues. Her nemesis is the "black magician" Harry:

> "How could you write that book? Are you so selfish? Are you so self-engrossed, you don't give a shit who you destroy? You told our whole story. All the details. You gave me away to my sister. Marvin's left me. He's gone."
> "Hey, it was loosely based on us."
> "Don't bullshit me, motherfucker. . . . I lived through it with you, okay? I know how loosely based it is."

Her indignation at being "given away" indicates the power of Harry's art to expose deception, but the virulence of the reaction indicates a sincere pain, anger, and sense of betrayal. In Lucy's accusation, Allen's recurring appreciation for magic conflates with Harry's corrosive aesthetic: "Now, two years later, your latest magnum opus emerges from this sewer of an apartment where you take everyone's suffering and turn it into gold, literary gold. Everyone's misery. You even *cause* their misery and mix your alchemy and turn it into gold. Like some fucking black magician!"

Harry's basement is a first reference to *Deconstructing Harry*'s structure of journey and descent. Confrontation occurs throughout, with virtually every "real" character—most centrally several ex-wives and a half-sister and her husband—cursing the writer for venomous betrayals/portrayals. The film ostensibly follows Harry's preparation for and journey to his former alma mater Adair University for an honoring ceremony. While this parallels the retrospective festival at the center of Sandy's experiences in *Stardust Memories* (1980), significant differences appear. In the later work the focus is not on the public film artist and the influence of his fans, but more narrowly on the private writer increasingly haunted by memories and the implications of his own paralyzing creative block. He confesses to the prostitute Cookie that "I'm spiritually bankrupt. I'm empty. . . . I'm frightened. I have no soul." As the movie progresses—Harry hunched over the wheel of his car, watery eyes forlorn and hopeless—his self-prognosis seems increasingly realized.

David Thomson offers a fascinating explication of Harry as Allen's representative persona:

> He shapes the climate in which he's always there ready to make a last effort to meet anyone's (cockamamie) ideas; . . . it's the credo that lets him think of himself as an endlessly patient, tolerant man, ready to talk about everything intelligently—especially the things that were most hurtful and irrational; and it's the mainstay of his self-pity, the way in which, whatever happens, whatever charges or bullets are hurled at him, whatever tirades slip like water from his sloped shoulders and elfin head, he's ready to be the sucker, the one who sits there and takes it, the victim.
>
> And this works well enough until, at last, you get a chance to look at him straight on and you see the bleakest eyes on today's screen, the intransigent certainty that it's all about *him*, and the passive resistance that knows if he keeps on asking in his listless, plaintive way, "What do you expect of me?", he doesn't have to deal with the question himself. (12)

Although Thomson veers close to an ad hominem attack on Allen, his analysis of Harry is compelling. Ironically, the protagonist's frustrated writing appears as much the source of his angst as the continual recriminations by those around him. When Harry's friend Richard evinces concern for his own faltering heart, he is abruptly interrupted: "Can I change the subject? Do you know I have writer's block?" Pat Dowell suggests that "the start of the nightmare journey" of *Stardust Memories* "surely comes to its bumpy end in *Deconstructing Harry*" (36). Harry's arrival at Adair is a symbolic culmination of his journey: in tow are a prostitute, a kidnapped son, and the body of Richard. As the author is welcomed by professors, a voice-over regarding the corpse seems applicable to Harry: "Is he alright?" someone asks. Cookie responds matter-of-factly: "He's dead, honey. You got one of them rubber bags?"

Moments later, like a character from his recent short story, Harry goes "out of focus." This confusion of reality and fantasy increases when the author describes to a group of Adair admirers that his next story involves a descent to hell. He makes one crucial qualification: "It's me thinly disguised. In fact, I don't even think I should disguise it anymore. It's me." What follows is the most harrowing fictional sequence of the film, and the only one in which Harry appears as "himself." This shift is already anticipated during the car trip. Apparent flashbacks begin to replace story scenes, signaling a blurring in Harry's mind between memory and fiction. The visit to hell is invention, and from its beginning a self-lacerating intent is clear: as Harry descends in an elevator to hell's lowest level, red lighting causes his "horn"-rim glasses—a physical staple of the Allen persona—to cast pointed shadows onto his forehead.

In the devil, Harry finds/creates a sympathetic counterpart. "Would you like a drink?" his host politely inquires. Harry notes that he "could be very comfortable here" and paraphrases Milton: "Better to rule down here than to serve in heaven." Harry discovers a metaphor ideally suited to the artist's hegemony: an underworld— subconscious? imagination? fictional artifact below common, accepted reality?—where many suffer for the enjoyment of the creator/destroyer. Despite its banter, quips, wisecracks, sarcasm, cleverness, and quick intelligence, the Harry/devil conversation is markedly not funny. The subject is sexual brutality; the tone is joyless. Harry explains why he is the more formidable of the two: "I'm more powerful because I'm a bigger sinner. Because you're a fallen angel, and I never believed in God, or heaven, or any of that stuff." The writer's choice of "evil," coupled with rejection of belief, exacerbates both culpability and power. When the devil concludes that, "One thing you're not, is a kidnapper," even he doesn't realize Harry's capabilities.

Throughout *Deconstructing Harry,* the writer's nihilism is considered in the context of artistic salvation. Harry's sister Dorris, frustrated by his abandonment of Jewish beliefs, laments that her brother "has no moral center. He's betting everything on physics and pussy." When Harry's second wife asks him if he's having more than one affair, Harry responds with ironic earnest:

"Amy Pollack was the only one. May God strike me dead if I'm lying."
"You're an Athiest, Harry."
"Hey, we're alone in the universe. You gonna blame that on me too?"

This exchange illustrates the writer's predicament: in the acceptance of nothingness, are the individual's acts without moral consequence or even more dependent on decency and fairness? Richard Blake sees this metaphysical dilemma as the central moral crisis from early in Allen's career: "if God does not exist, then the human person, as an individual, becomes the sole measure of the good, but the universe as a whole is meaningless and human actions, however heroic and altruistic, are likewise meaningless" (23). Harry is resigned to bleak godlessness. Only the artist as creator remains, a crucial element absent from Dorris's list of what Harry's "betting on."

The idea of salvation for the artist through the immortality of writing has frequently meet with Allen's skepticism. "Some artists think that art will save them, that they will be immortalized through their art, they will live on through their art. But the truth of the matter is, art doesn't save you. . . . I mean, it doesn't profit Shakespeare one iota that his plays have lived on after him. He would have been better off if he was alive and his plays were forgotten" (*Woody* 103). This sentiment seems supported in the film. Harry returns from his fictional hell to the Adair campus, asking saliently, "Can't I be honored and then arrested?" A peculiar sequence follows, when in his jail cell Harry is visited by Richard's ghost. This event is not presented as fiction, implying either an increasingly hallucinatory mind or, more incongruously, that Richard is a "real" supernatural figure. He serves as confessor, one privy to information beyond Harry's earth-bound knowledge. While not disagreeing with the writer's pained, "I'm no good at life," Richard adds that Harry creates a universe "much nicer than the world we have" and that his stories "bring pleasure to a lot of people. That's good." Only this appraisal—supported by the peripheral praises of Adair faculty and students—testifies to the value of Harry's work to anyone beyond himself. Otherwise, the film's persistent focus is on the author's inability to live in the present world and the effect of this on his subjects. Richard, sad and elusive concerning the afterlife—and a resident of the real hell?—ends with an enigmatic comment equally warning and advice: "To be alive is to be happy. Take it from me."

Richard's appearance as apparition marks a significant variation in the film's pattern. Earlier, Harry's calmest conversations are with his characters. These first occur when the trip is briefly delayed for a visit to a local fair. This sequence—with its addition of Allen's nearly requisite "magic"—also involves the initial moment Harry participates in a flash-back/fiction. Afterwards, he meets and fails to recognize his fictionalized self, Ken. "Look at this guy. You created me, now you don't recognize me? . . . I'm just you, thinly disguised. You gave me a little more maturity, and a different name." Harry's characters claim more knowledge of the author than he himself holds, perhaps linking the creation of art to an opening of unconscious awareness otherwise inaccessible. This pre-science goes further when Ken allows Harry to watch an actual scene between sisters Jane and Lucy, one from which the author was absent. Similarly, Harry's creation Helen later escorts him to a private conversation between Dorris and her husband Burt. "You can't fool me," Ken explains. "I'm not like your shrink. He only knows what you tell him. I know the truth." The film never subverts or contradicts the "authority" of Harry's characters, suggesting an odd re-inversion of fiction as reality and provocatively asserting the artist's powers as beyond his control.

However, self-knowledge in *Deconstructing Harry* is inadequate to initiate profound change. In Terrence Rafferty's judgment, "forgiving yourself—in the name of art—for betraying love and trust of other people may well have major therapeutic value. It's *moral* value, however, is precisely zero" (126). Many critics interpreted *Deconstructing Harry* as a nearly unqualified endorsement of the artist's self-indulgence and transcendence of "ordinary" values. Some of this confusion may stem from Allen's professed love of writing and fantasy. "In real life, people disappoint you. They're cruel, and life is cruel. And if you choose reality over fantasy, which you must, you have to pay the price for it" ("Human" 32). Allen, an obsessive workaholic, takes a regenerative attitude toward the value of art for the creator. "I've never re-evaluated my life! I've always kept my nose to the grindstone. All I do is work, and my philosophy has always been that if I just keep working, just focus on my work, everything else will fall into place" (*Woody* 192). For the characters in Allen's films, retreat into fantasy most often manifests as film viewing. However, to accept fantasy in place of life and not merely as solace is to fall prey to delusion and even psychosis. "But innocence is fiction," Allen explains in reference to *The Purple Rose of Cairo,* his fullest exploration of the relationship between audience and film fantasy, with the latter's enticements, seductions, dangers, and ultimate impossibility. "We can't live that kind of innocence" (*Woody* 151). Cecilia in that film has, finally, "to choose the real world," although romance is punctured by the departure of the actor Gil. "It ain't the movies. It's real life," her abusive husband warns. Still, the film's bittersweet ending is invested with Cecilia's hard-won independence.

Harry errs in an opposite direction from Cecilia, into chronic habitation of his self-sustaining revisions. "Allen isn't willing to translate Harry's involvement with art into even a tentative step toward functioning in the real world" (37) Michael Kerbel asserts. Leonard Quart further assesses the film's troubling conclusion:

> Still, if the film suggests that Harry's being a successful artist absolves him from ordinary moral standards . . . it hesitates endorsing this megalomaniacal, self-justifying notion. Allen has Harry experience the melancholy self-knowledge that the only time people applaud him in the film occurs in his fantasy life. Consequently, the film's climax leaves Harry with nothing but his work—a far from triumphant image. He's only happy bent over his writing. . . . The finale leaves Harry stripped down and alone—a direct admission of human failure. (34)

Harry is rescued from jail by his friend (and fictional devil) Larry and his lost love Faye, the latter nearly the only person not brutalized in his fiction. Otherwise, he is absolved only by his characters. "I give up. I give up," he says, and *Deconstructing Harry*'s last scene shows Harry alone with his typewriter. "Everyone is waiting to honor you," announces an Adair professor now part of the writer's fantasy. The camera pans across the smiling fictions of those Harry has angered and revealed. "I love you all," he announces. "You've given me some of the happiest moments of my life." The scene constitutes Harry's triumph, but only as delusional dream. The moment's pathos is overriding. Ironically, it is Harry's most sympathetic depiction.

In *Bullets Over Broadway* (1994), David Shayne's acceptance of his failure as a writer is finally empowering and redemptive, a movement into the risky, cruel, but rewarding world of the human. "There are two things of which I'm certain: one is that I love you. And two is that I'm not an artist. There, I said it, and I feel fine. I'm not an artist. Will you marry me?" The ambivalence that Allen brings in *Deconstructing Harry* to his treatment of the artist's neurosis and the cost of high fantasy is underscored by these two films' radically different conclusions. Closing an endless circle of self-referentiality that moves him ever-further from the real world, Harry's ceremony returns him to work. The secret to his release from writer's block—an ailment tantamount to disappearance or death—is deeper fantasy. "I like it. I like it. A character who's too neu-rotic to function in life, but can only function in art." As Harry begins notes for a novel, the scene's jump cuts recall Lucy at the film's begin-ning. "Ripken led a fragmented, disjointed existence. He had long ago come to this conclusion: All people know the same truth. Our lives con-sist of how we choose to distort it." His words echo Sherwood Ander-son's "The Book of the Grotesque." The dark implications of Harry's recovery are fully in his view, but disregarded by necessity. Escape is not desired. The writer moves deeper into another rite of consuming re-cre-ation, and jerky editing gives way to visual fluidity, to the soothing conti-nuity and control of fiction. "Only his writing was calm. His writing, which had in more ways than one, saved his life." Harry is where he be-longs, typing, the steering wheel of his "real" odyssey replaced. The black magician is back in the basement.

In her recent study *Reconstructing Woody,* Mary P. Nichols argues that those who routinely conflate Allen with his on-screen personae—often savagely since the filmmaker's controversies of the early 1990s—fall for an intentional joke in *Deconstructing Harry:* "for Allen has given his most vociferous critics . . . a version of the despicable person they imagine that he is. . . . But to identify Allen with one of his characters is to confuse biography and fiction, life and art—one of the errors that the movie shows Harry making. Indeed, this is one of the worst things Harry does" (x). Graham McCann argued in 1990 that "the more successful Allen's movies became, the less free he was to experiment with his screen persona" (142), which if true makes *Deconstructing Harry* an even more radical departure— daring, elusive, and full of land mines for critics. Allen the actor is absent from his next film, *Celebrity,* released less than a year later, but Kenneth Branagh gives "a dead-on imperson-ation" (Rainer, "Empty" 121). The film emerges as an intriguing com-panion to its predecessor, a further study of a writer struggling to deal with the real world of individuals and ethical responsibilities.

Celebrity is a sort of inverted *Stardust Memories* (that the more re-cent film is shot in black and white further links the two). The first movie raised questions about the artist's relationship with his fans, but held hope in the protagonist's continuation "perhaps always futilely, trying to make some sense of things" (Pogel 149). *Celebrity* concerns a writer closer to being a fan than to becoming a successful *auteur*, an ambitious sycophant whose identity is lost in a swirl of celebrity glitz. The film constitutes for Richard Schickel "a screen version of Thackeray's *Vanity Fair* or some other satirical, multilayered saga of halfway decent,

halfway desperate people trying to make their way into a corrupt society" (104). The salutary effects of cinema for lonely viewers—found in
The Purple Rose of Cairo and so many Allen films—is subsumed by the
frenzy of greed, lust, and fear on the other side of the screen. *Celebrity*
deals with makers and players, the seemingly arbitrary nature of success
in a predatory world, and the debilitating effect of attempted participa-
tion by an individual without luck or a compass of integrity.

Protagonist Lee Simon's screenplay in *Celebrity*, an armored-car
potboiler called *The Heist,* is a product ready to be mutilated by its author to interest any bankable actor. Much of the humor of Lee's interaction with stars involves this absurdly compromised project. He informs a
sexy starlet that the "there's room for a real feminist statement" with the
script—as soon as he rewrites one of the guards to be a woman. In an ex-
tended sequence, self-consumed actor Brandon Darrow alternately encourages and destroys a project to which Lee has devoted a year, all
revisions dictated by whim. "Character development. . . . Who is this guy
Sonny Boy? . . . Why does he need to score so bad? Know what I'm saying?" Afterwards, Lee craps out at a casino table. Brandon takes his roll
and, predictably, wins. When Lee attempts an oblique praise of his own
work, he is immediately deflated. "I was wondering how you felt about
the way I handled the robbery. 'Cause I think it's just a terrific sequence.
I'm very happy about it." Brandon squeaks from a lungful of marijuana,
"Needs a complete rewrite," and the author agrees "it needs some work."
Richard Schickel notes that the protagonist "subsists emotionally on
such crusts . . . as the famous discard as they pass by. . . . They can smell
his desperation. It invites their contempt" (104). Peter Rainer defines
Lee's personality as "both fawning and acrid—the perfect hack combo"
("Empty" 121).

Clearly, *The Heist* holds no esthetic merit. It is the vehicle by which
Lee hopes to ingratiate his way to prestige and fame. *Celebrity* posits a
society driven wild by its own gaze, "a world of gorgeous poseurs"
where "the centrifugal force of celebrity sucks up everything in its path"
(Travers 131). Dr. Lupus, a plastic surgeon made famous by a *Newsweek*
article, is "an artist" who recreates his patients in an image of media/Hol-
lywood perfection. A supplicant asks priest and television star Father
Glavin, "Who would you say is more popular, the Pope or Elvis Pres-
ley?" The question is rhetorical. Celebrity infects all aspects of intro-
spection, reverie, individuality, and personal integrity. The demotic
consumes both secular and sacred. Guest cameos dot the film's landscape. Donald Trump informs us his new project is to buy and destroy St.

Patrick's cathedral, "doing a little rip down job and putting up a very very tall and beautiful building." The moment is funny and terrible. Gossip is truth, and physical beauty is religion. Lee gibbers to a distracted supermodel: "If the universe has any meaning at all, I'm looking at it. . . . You're a miracle." Her most enthusiastic response of the evening is, "Look at your Astin Martin!"

Fame is the putative blessing granted or withheld in *Celebrity*. Lee suffers from a spiritual malaise the source of which, remarkably, he cannot seem to determine. He offers his wife Robin little reason for abandoning their marriage, relying instead on clichés—"It's me. I'm confused. I want a different life. I want to go in a different direction."— and ending with the childlike repetition, "I'm not happy. I'm not happy." In a second flashback, the apparent genesis of the breakup is revealed in an epiphanic moment at Lee's class of 1975 high school reunion. Over the strains of "The Impossible Dream," performed by lounge singer Monroe Gordon, the class "celebrity," Lee surveys his former classmates and sees a horrifying reflection of himself. "And Freddie Kaplan's my age. He could easily be my father's pinochle partner." Lee mutters to himself of "fucking Prufrock," then continues the literary analogy: "I just turned forty. I don't want to look up at fifty and find I measured out my fucking life with a coffee spoon." His evaluation employs a literary text even while stating its vapid dream: "I don't want to spend my life the wife of a school teacher . . . never knowing what it's like to make love to that amazing, sleazy blonde that's married to Monroe Gordon. . . . You see, I don't know what the truth is anymore. . . . Ask not for whom the bells tolls, or, more accurately, ask not for whom the toilet flushes."

Celebrity is littered with literary references. These are routinely dismissed, mocked, or assimilated. During an orgy initiated by the star Brandon, Lee's bimbo partner informs him that she too is a writer: "I wrote some film scripts. . . . You ever heard of Chekhov? . . . I write like him." When his wife Robin tells producer Tony Gardella —a smart man who nevertheless fails to recognize her impression of Blanche DuBois in their initial meeting at Dr. Lupus's—that "all I'm good at is Chaucer," he responds with tongue-in-cheek aplomb: "Well, we have a cooking show. You could do great writers' recipes. Chaucer's fettucini with clam sauce, Sir Walter Raleigh's gazpacho." For Lee, the high school reunion appears momentous, but the invocation of Eliot and Donne serves only as erudite decoration for libido. In practice, his new life is hustling *The Heist*. However, *Celebrity* implies that Lee fails not because his ambitions are avaricious and shallow—this merely aligns him with nearly everyone in the movie— but because he is capable of something better, work and behavior that would enable personal dignity and artistic fulfillment. This potential he habitually betrays.

Lee's humiliating antics so well cloak his literary ambitions that it is well into the film before Allen reveals that the protagonist is a frustrated novelist. The information is relayed as admonishment from supporter/mentor Bonnie. "I think you should forget about all that screenplay nonsense and get back to writing your novel." Bonnie, an editor, represents a literary world of serious, individual achievement, a world in *Celebrity* partially in contrast to the tinsel of popular celebrity. In this context, Lee's persistence with his screenplay signals an insecurity about his own talent that approaches self-loathing: "Maybe after I sell my armored car robbery script, then, you know, I'll get back to something more serious." His voice communicates that even to Lee such an assertion is veiled cowardice. Bonnie encourages him nevertheless:

> "Are you telling me you'll never get over some bad reviews?"
> "My two novels were dismissed. It was brutal. Maybe after I
> sell a screenplay. Film is where it's at. I mean, who reads books
> anymore, anyway? Not young kids. They're into cinema."
> "I don't believe that and neither do you."

Only two moments in *Celebrity* show Lee impassioned and confident, and the contrast of scenes is illuminating. In the first, Bonnie escorts him to a party of high-power literary figures. Lee announces that he is "out of [his] league" and "awash in self-contempt." As the evening progresses, drinks pour, Lee reminisces over literary influences, and his usual self-doubt momentarily subsides. In the sad, generous eyes of the editor Philip, Lee comes alive. He speaks of his novel and his culture with passion and surety. "My book is about the values of a society gone astray. A culture badly in need of help. A country that gives a twenty-year-old kid who can barely read or write a hundred-million-dollar contract to play basketball?! Or where a brutal murder trial, or who's sleeping with the president, it's all show business. Everything's show business!" The comments are de facto a dismissal of the society to which he has craved entry. Lee glows; he is an artist of integrity and courage, with verve and incisive viewpoints. Philip too encourages him to finish the novel. "Screenplays have their place. But I mean, it's nothing like a serious book." Allen's comic undercutting, by a nearby critic who lambasted Lee's first novel, doesn't erase the image of a man briefly transformed.

However, like all others in *Celebrity,* the literary world is co-opted by media and marketing. Nearly everyone in the film seems to be writing something, and little practical distinction is made between screenplay, article, or novel. Lee's moment at the party, free from self-promotion and sales strategies, is unique. Even Bonnie later sells a screenplay. Wherever the rare individual artist may be, he is not in the lights of the paparazzi and his audience is small. For a while, Lee returns to the novel: "I guess I just woke up. . . . I reread what I'd written. Well, you know, they contain every aspiration that I've had. Every authentic, um, feeling, every idea. And I got no choice, I have to complete this. This is me. I love this book. I love this book."

Ironically, the confidence Lee gains from the apparent return of imaginative force manifests as a betraying self-conceit. Although Stanley Kauffmann oddly identifies the character of Lee Simon as "essentially the recently deconstructed Harry under another name" ("Doodling" 26), one scene in *Celebrity* does recall Harry's confusion between fiction and life. Lee's meeting with the waitress Nola, at a kiosk at midnight—"Can I make you a more European offer?" she asks—finds him riding a crest of creative and sexual assurance. His speech is fluid and forceful; lacking are the stutters of his customary begging. "Twice you were the obscure object of desire in books that I've written," he informs her. In a film conspicuously missing Allen's usual flourishes of fantasy or magic—as if the flash of cameras blinds the quiet possibility of supernatural grace—Lee momentarily enjoys an omniscience indistinguishable from the fiction writer's. In Nola, he has an audience ready to believe.

> "Yeah, well what am I thinking?"
> "You're thinking I wish this guy would shut up and kiss me. . . .
> Except, you know, why would I kiss you here when your apartment is two blocks away?"
> "How did you know that?"
> "Well, why wouldn't I know where you live? You were Stephanie in my first book, and Louise in my second, and now—you're Nola."

The scene ends with swelling music and a romantic movie kiss.

Bolstered by Bonnie's support, Lee employs his renewed prowess to engineer his betrayal of her. "I know you're gonna think I'm like the worst, most fucked-up son of a bitch in the world, and I am." His revelation arrives even as moving men deliver Bonnie's furniture. Unlike

Harry—perhaps because Lee has remnants of guilt and decency, perhaps because he is artistically compromised or lacking in talent—Lee cannot complete a proper fictional world for himself. His "fictionalized" betrayal with Nola takes place in the real world and inadvertently obliterates any hope for his sustained rejuvenation. Moments after his attempt "to be honest," he watches as Bonnie, on a distant and dwindling ferry, scatters the pages of his novel manuscript onto indifferent waves. The relationship with Nola soon proves to be the fiction that he first recognizes, and, like Harry, Lee finally greets failed relationships and personal defeat with the admission, "I give up."

The conclusion of *Celebrity* takes place at the premiere of a Hollywood blockbuster satirically entitled *The Liquidator.* When Lee and Robin accidentally meet for the second time, again at a movie opening, their fortunes have shifted. Robin is transformed into a bleached-blonde gossip-show host, the bland world of Chaucer behind her. Lee immediately recognizes the internal change.

> "Have I become insufferable?"
> "No. You look very happy. Confident, and radiant."

She instructs Lee that "when it comes to love, it's luck," and hopes that he will "catch a break." Allen's film frequently mentions luck, both good and bad. More surprising is the focus on simple and redemptive love. Graham Fuller attributes the characters' reversals to a notion that "love is possible if celebrity . . . isn't a component of it," and "the need to get into bed with celebrity occurs in the absence of love and self-esteem" (63). Robin and Tony, munching popcorn and smiling, seem out of place in a film ostensibly concerning fame and power. Richard Schickel analyzes Robin's happy ascent: "The pilgrim's path is made easier, Allen says, if he or she is armored by innocence rather than made vulnerable by naked need. It also helps if there is someone utterly indifferent to fame who can lend a guiding hand" (104).

Celebrity ends with a projection of the film being made at its beginning. A camera surveys the audience of *The Liquidator,* some of whom, like actress Nicole Oliver, we recognize as characters from the film we have just watched. Unlike the ending of *Deconstructing Harry,* however, they are not the protagonist's creations. Lee also sits in the audience, staring at a Hollywood skywriting of "Help" as if it were his fading, personal plea. Allen summarizes the theme of his earlier study of stardom, *Stardust Memories*: Sandy "came to the conclusion that there are just some moments in life—that's all you have in life are moments, not your artistic achievements, not your material goods, not your fame or your money—just some moments, maybe another person, . . . those little moments that are wonderful" (Pogel 148). The close of *Celebrity* shares the poignancy of the earlier film's conclusion, but with the writer's future even more tenuous. Returned to the margins of celebrated society, Lee has neither Robin's "little moments" nor the integrity—nor, like Harry Block, the refuge—of artistic creation. However, he seems sincerely happy for his ex-wife's success, humbled by his own need, and profoundly alone is a world of movie gods. Lee Simon, we sense, will be neither an artist nor a star, and we leave him alone in the dark. But perhaps, through humility and grace, his luck will turn. He seems by the film's end to have begun a painful journey back to simple, humanizing values.

In his earlier film *Alice* (1990), Allen suggests that the failure of the creative/artistic spirit is not necessarily indicative of irredeemable spiritual collapse. Like Lee Simon, Alice realizes her internal emptiness needs attention: "I want to do something with my life before it's too late." However, her dedication to a writing life is never convincing in the film, only another tentative experiment. "I wrote when I was a kid. I always loved poetry and drama," she tells her husband Doug. She pitches ideas to friend Nancy Brill, but the autobiographical stories are too tame for television. After a first tryst with her lover Joe, Alice appears in a creative writing class, "a clear indication that she has gained the courage to move out of Doug's orbit intellectually as well as sexually" (Blake 194). The most important attribute Alice seems to lack as a writer—possibly aside from talent and determination—is toughness. Even Alice's saucy muse is skeptical: "You're not psychological at all. How are you going to be a writer?" Peter Rainer adduces that, like Cecilia in *The Purple Rose of Cairo,* Alice "seems almost too fragile for this world" ("Review" 37).

Alice's aspirations as a writer wither because her journey is one of self-discovery; the fictionalizing of those around her is useless and impossible until a victory of personal knowledge. Anticipating the conclusion of *Bullets Over Broadway,* Allen has Alice's recognition of her failure as an artist signal a beginning. "I can't write. And if I could, I'm incapable of a thought larger than a TV plot." She culminates this release from art's demands—irrelevant to her needs—by announcing that she is going to Calcutta to work with Mother Teresa. Critics debated the abrupt and apparently unironized conclusion of *Alice.* Jonathan Romney contends that the character has merely selected one illusion over another, and that her "future may still exist purely in her own imagination" (38). Regardless of the merits of its outcome, Alice's journey is therapeutic rather than esthetic/creative. Allen explains that the mystical Dr. Yang creates a fanciful, accelerated psychoanalysis for the protagonist: "she's really doing the same thing, working with her creative impulses, her dreams, past memories of relationships" ("Clip" 57). Unlike Harry Block, who turns inward to control the world, Alice turns outward. Unlike Lee Simon, she escapes, with the assistance of Dr. Yang's potent "herbs," the allure of popular writing.

Marcia Pally elaborates that even when the writer's work is not central to a film's theme, Allen encourages fiction to his audience by his characters' habitual escape into magic, fantasy, and imagination.

> Yet Allen recognizes that cynicism is too harsh a vision by which to live, agnosticism is insufficient, and so people construct fictions to soothe loss and doubt. . . . When Allen's films are not overtly about fiction, they are object lessons that recommend it. He scripts predicaments that would be disasters in life and gives them happy movie endings. . . . Going along with the story of movies or myth is already a leap into faith. Suspension of disbelief is belief nonetheless. (33)

Even Allen acknowledges that "one big theme" appears in his films, "the difference between fantasy and reality" (*Woody* 50). Two recent offerings charmingly interweave fiction and reality, demonstrating skills of a writer/director far beyond the hackneyed (Lee) or cannibalizing (Harry) efforts of the filmmaker's fictional counterparts.

Manhattan Murder Mystery (1993) cleverly tailors the metaphor of the mystery to its concern with middle-aged angst and tired marriage. Having compulsively leapt into a possible murder case, Carol announces herself "just dizzy with freedom. This is just the craziest thing I've ever done." Her friend Ted explains: "Yes, it's crazy. Soon we'll be too old to do anything crazy." Kent Jones notes that the film "plays on the insularity that runs through the rest of [Allen's] movies as an unsettling subtext" (6). For Carol, the perceived murder is escapist adventure, a fantasy that overtakes reality and engulfs even her husband (a publisher, therefore blasé toward vicarious fictions). "Larry, is this the most exciting things that's ever happened to us in our whole marriage?" she asks. He finally succumbs: "I will never say that life doesn't imitate art again." The generic plot of *Manhattan Murder Mystery* serves the film's theme of the slippery relation between life and art. Larry ultimately "recognizes that he is wrong, that his wife really is into a mystery; this amounts to a recognition that the ideal is connected to the real, or art to life. That the romance and adventure of sleuthing can be embodied in a marriage thus serves as an illustration of how art can inform life" (Nichols 170). Despite Sander H. Lee's understandable skepticism about whether the resolution of the crime signals a "fundamental or permanent" (340) reconciliation between Larry and Carol, the ameliorative, sustaining effect of art on life is nevertheless the film's concluding assertion.

Finally, what is the viewer to make of the fanciful *Everyone Says I Love You* (1995), Allen's film prior to *Deconstructing Harry*? The musical brims with charm, inspired whimsy, and legitimate feelings of loss, sadness, and affection. "I'm through with love," is the film's musical mantra, yet its title reveals a different impulse: the touching, unending, hesitant reaching of its characters toward embrace. Joe Berlin is another novelist, but we learn little of his approach or his talent. Chastised by his ex-wife Steffi—their mutual affection identifies them as unique in Allen's oeuvre—because he didn't know if he "wanted to be a psychoanalyst or a writer," Joe offers a waggish modification: "So I compromised. I became a writer and a patient." Again, the shift is toward therapy, self-analysis, and a lifetime's gradual understanding. "Funny how life goes," Steffi ponders. Joe can only respond, "It's amazing, amazing." Earlier, their daughter DJ announces, "It's later than you think," and Joe's last lines corroborate: "Definitely late. Christmas Eve and late. Let's go." *Everyone Says I Love You* is a melancholy film; it evokes the sad joy of family, holidays, and tender connections. Graham McCann contends that "what remains for Woody Allen is the 'problem' of other people. Allen's heroes have come to realize that there is no 'correct' response to Tracy's comment in *Manhattan* about having a little faith in people; our faith always was, and is, so terribly, awfully fragile" (246).

In *Everyone Says I Love You,* the lovely Von has a dream she reveals only in therapy: "I'm in the elevator. And it just keeps going up, and up, and up." Joe, perhaps with a writer's callousness, exploits this secret information. One can't help notice, however, the hopeful way in which he tries to fulfill Von's Paris dream/fiction. Joe's goal is the inverse of the novelist's. His fantasy-weaving attempts to improve the world, but still to live within it and to ingratiate author to subject: "I've been playing this character just to win you over, to get you to like me, to make you happy." The meaning of her dream is not known. However, unlike Harry Block's ride to his own hell, Von's movement is ascent, a rising into a world of openness and possibilities. Inevitably, the relationship fails, and the end of *Everyone Says I Love You* leaves Joe without a country or a foreseeable future. Despite Woody Allen's obsession with writing and his recommendation of fiction for comfort, an ambivalence toward the creative act lingers in his films. The writer is the architect of his constructed world. He may succeed in creating a convincing land of characters, but that place will prove lonely if he has no one else.

Note

The author thanks Middle Tennessee State University for the Non-Instructional Assignment that allowed the completion of this essay. Also, thank you to Jennifer Thornton, MTSU Interlibrary Loan, for emergency assistance.

Works Cited

Allen, Woody. "Film Clip: Woody Allen." Interview by Roger Ebert. *The Woody Allen Companion.* 55–59 Ed. Stephen J. Spignesi. Kansas City: Andrews and McMeel, 1992. First published in *Roger Ebert's Movie Home Companion.*

———. "Human Existence with a Penthouse View." Interview by Stephen Farber. . 30-38. *The Woody Allen Companion.* Ed. Stephen J. Spignesi. Kansas City: Andrews and McMeel, 1992. First published in *Moviegoers* May 1985.

———. *Woody Allen on Woody Allen.* Interviews by Stig Björkman. New York: Grove, 1993.

Ansen, David. "Movies: Season of the Grinch." *Newsweek* 22 Dec. 1997, 84–86.

Blake, Richard A. *Woody Allen: Profane and Sacred.* Lanham, MD: Scarecrow, 1995.

Dowell, Pat. "Woody's Effort to Reconstruct Himself." (Part of "Deconstructing Woody: A Critical Symposium on Woody Allen's *Deconstructing Harry*," 32–38.) *Cineaste* Summer 1998, 35–36.

Fuller, Graham. "Ready for the Eighth Deadly Sin?" *Interview* Nov. 1998, 63.

Girgus, Sam B. *The Films of Woody Allen.* Cambridge: Cambridge University Press, 1993.

Jones, Kent. "Into the Woods." *Film Comment* May-June 1998, 4–6.

Kauffmann, Stanley. "Doodling and Delving." *New Republic* 21 Dec. 1998, 26.

—— "New York Jews." *New Republic* 19 Jan 1998, 24.

Kerbel, Michael. "The Redemptive Power of Art." (Part of "Deconstructing Woody: A Critical Symposium on Woody Allen's *Deconstructing Harry*," 32–38.) *Cineaste* Summer 1998, 36–7.

Lax, Eric. *On Being Funny: Woody Allen and Comedy.* New York: Charterhouse, 1975.

Lee, Sander H. *Woody Allen's Angst.* Jefferson, NC: McFarland, 1997.

McCann, Graham. *Woody Allen: New Yorker.* Cambridge: Polity, 1990.

Nichols, Mary P. *Reconstructing Woody: Art, Love, and Life in the Films of Woody Allen.* Lanham, MD: Rowman & Littlefield, 1998.

Pally, Marcia. "The Cinema as Secular Religion." (Part of "Deconstructing Woody: A Critical Symposium on Woody Allen's *Deconstructing Harry*," 32–38.) *Cineaste* Summer 1998, 32–3.

Pogel, Nancy. *Woody Allen.* Boston: Twayne, 1987.

Quart, Leonard. "Woody Allen's Reflexive Critics." (Part of "Deconstructing Woody: A Critical Symposium on Woody Allen's *Deconstructing Harry*," 32–38.) *Cineaste* Summer 1998, 34–5.

Rafferty, Terrence. "Hauteur Theory." *GQ* Mar. 1998, 125+.

Rainer, Peter. "Movies: Running on Empty." *New York* 30 Nov. 1998, 121.

——. Rev. of *Alice. Film Review Annual 1991.* 37–38. Eaglewood, NJ: Jerome S. Ozer, 1991. First published in *Los Angeles Times* 25 Dec. 1990: Calendar 1+.

Romney, Jonathan. Rev. of *Alice. Sight and Sound* July 1991, 37–38.

Schickel, Richard. "The Wages of Fame." *Time* 16 Nov. 1998, 104–5.

Thomson, David. "Shoot the Actor." *Film Comment* Mar.-Apr. 1998, 12+.

Travers, Peter. "Woody Allen Plays the Fame Game." *Rolling Stone* 26 Nov. 1998, 131–132.

Yacowar, Maurice. *Loser Take All: The Comic Art of Woody Allen.* New York: Frederick Ungar, 1979.

Art Devours Life in Woody Allen's *Deconstructing Harry*

JOHN BICKLEY

Every once in a while Woody Allen reminds us that he is a genius. Over the decades, his compulsive work ethic and almost complete artistic autonomy have been the drive and device for the production of over thirty films. Though his American audience has diminished in number over the years and most of his films pass quietly through the theaters, every once and awhile, even mainstream America recognizes in Woody a sensibility, both comic and tragic, and an artistic maturity that function on a higher level than the dull round to which it has become inured.

Like any mature artist, his work is unmistakable. The modest opening titles, naturalistic dialog, subversive humor, overcast settings, and fragmented storylines—replete with flashbacks, mock interviews, and anecdotes—have become the distinct stylistic trademarks of a Woody Allen film. This style has developed along with his similarly unmistakable thematic concerns. Allen struggles with the same questions now as he did in the beginning of his career. Even in his stand-up routine of the mid-sixties, Allen wrestled with such themes as the meaninglessness in life and death, the existence or nonexistence of God, the limits of love, the potentials of love, psychoanalysis and the modern psyche, neurosis and psychosis, fidelity and lack thereof, and the artist and his or her interactions with reality. It is in the struggle with such themes, and the way in which he expresses this struggle, that we see the genius of Woody's emotive and artistic sensibility.

The theme of the artist and his struggle to deal with reality is one of Allen's more prevalent and complex themes. After his relationship with

Soon-Yi Previn became public in '92, this theme becomes even more poignant and personal. Though Allen addresses the same theme in such works as *Annie Hall* (1977), *Stardust Memories* (1980), *The Purple Rose of Cairo* (1985), *Hannah and Her Sisters* (1986), and *Bullets Over Broadway* (1994), he does not confront it in the head-on, comprehensive manner that he does in his 1997 film *Deconstructing Harry*. In this film, begun three years after the breaking of the Soon-Yi news story, Allen struggles, once again, with questions about the personal life of an artist and his inability to come to terms with reality. Allen develops this theme through the tone, cinematic techniques and, most notably, the disjointed and ironic storyline of the film, but this time Allen's approach would be far different.

Deconstructing Harry centers on the chaotic life of Harry Block, an acclaimed novelist who is completely unable to live any sort of ordered life outside of his fiction. Harry just can't seem to figure out how to function in society—how to conform to conventional moral standards, marriage vows, and basic laws of decency. Harry's life is a mess. He has written his friends and family right out of his life. He has sabotaged in one way or another at least four marriages—three of his own and one of his sister-in-law's. His last wife has custody of their son, and all the women at the elementary school think he's the devil incarnate. His sister is still unable to get over the insulting caricature he wrote of her in one of his books; his ex-sister-in-law wants to murder him. And to make matters worse, he's got an obstinate case of writer's block. With these given circumstances, anything could and does happen—including one particularly funny car ride with a prostitute named Cookie, Harry's (kidnapped) son, and Harry's old friend, Richard, who dies tragically before they arrive at the college.

But the film is no light comedy. On the contrary, at times it is bitter and abrasive. The lead character, Harry, played almost too perfectly by Woody Allen, is undoubtedly funny, but he is also repulsive in his moral deficiencies. The language of the film, unlike most of Allen's other work, is explicitly profane. The jump-cuts and flashbacks and fictional reenactments are unnerving—almost schizophrenic. The sex is anything but romantic, the characters all degraded, the plotline jagged and disordered, the nudity gratuitous, the ending flaccid and unsettling. Allen's film is a disturbing mixture of humor, bitterness, and depravity. This conflicted tone is discordant and unsettling, but it is also perfect in that it mirrors the mental state of Harry, as he watches his life unravel. In this way, Allen allows the audience to get inside the conflicted psyche of his character.

Allen portrays the character of Harry not only through tone, but also through the disjointed plotline of the film. Many of Allen's films appear directionless. The storylines of *Annie Hall, Manhattan* (1979), *Zelig* (1983), *Radio Days* (1987), and *Celebrity* (1998) skip from scene to scene, creating a feeling of a haphazard manner of narration. This is largely due to Allen's distinctive style of anachronistic, episodic story-lines. Depending upon the subject matter and themes of the film, this "di-rectionless" narrative technique can be viewed as either a strength or a weakness. In the case of *Annie Hall*, for instance, the feeling of direc-tionlessness is appropriate for the neurotic tone of the film. In *Celebrity*, the story is difficult to follow at times, cutting from one scene to the next, very often promoting only confusion in my mind.

The plotline of *Deconstructing Harry* could be diagnosed as schizo-phrenic. The frequent use of jump-cuts and sudden shifts from the pre-sent narrative into flashbacks, fictional digressions, and eventually hallucinations are symptoms of a neurotic storyline—a perfect affliction for the story of Harry Block. The film begins with an episode from Harry's most recent publication. We as the audience, of course, do not know this, and just as we begin to get used to the characters presented, the story jumps into Harry's "sewer" of an apartment. Lucy enters and so begins her foul-mouthed diatribe, rebuking him for his latest selfish and destructive novel. By the end of her verbal assault, Lucy has moved to a more physical remonstrance; she holds Harry at gunpoint on the roof of his apartment building. Harry begins to desperately tell her about the story he is currently revising, and, suddenly, the scene jumps back into the fictional world of Harry Block. Halfway through this narrative, con-cerning a young man named Harvey Stern and his unfortunate run-in with Death, we find ourselves in the office of Harry's analyst. The movie continues in this manner, leaping back and forth from fiction to reality, from present to past.

In this disconnected narrative technique, Allen masterfully depicts the disorder of Harry's life. As the story progresses, we find that Harry's fictional creations have virtually destroyed his life. His latest novel dis-mantled Lucy's marriage. His story about one of his ex-wives wrecked his relationship with his sister. His on-going love affair with his own work undermined his real life affair with Faye. The more we learn about Harry Block, the more we see the destructive nature of his art.

As has been stated, what is so impressive in this ranting tantrum of a movie is the bold reassessment of a theme that appears in several of Allen's preceding films. *Deconstructing Harry* takes this theme and addresses it from an abrasive and ironic point of view. The relationship of the artist to reality is a subject frequently confronted by Allen. Even in his early films, Allen examines the artist's interactions with reality, the artist's role in society, and the role of art in the life of the artist. Over the years, the same subject matter has proved elusive and inexhaustible— with Allen finding different answers every time he looks. For example, in *Annie Hall* Allen presents art as a means of coming to terms with reality, a saving grace. Art is, to Alvy Singer, an anaesthetic that makes the pains of life bearable. After the final break up with Annie in L.A., Alvy writes a play (his first) based upon their relationship. The writing of the play is Alvy's means of accepting the reality of the break up. Though never fully able to heal any wounds, art is portrayed here as capable of relieving much of the discomforts of reality. In *Hannah and Her Sisters*, Holly finally finds a sense of direction and identity in writing. In this case, art is redemptive and the artist finds fulfillment in the creation of art. Interestingly, she also announces her pregnancy, as if it were a metaphor for her own new life.

Deconstructing Harry takes this theme of the artist and reality and depicts it in a bitter and severe light. Instead of art as a means of reconciliation with reality, as found in both *Annie Hall* and *Hannah*, Harry's art seems to do nothing but separate him from his loved ones. Instead of redeeming him, Harry's art creates his major problems. Though his fiction is praised by even his most antipathetic of relationships, there seems to be no positive, personal benefits: all of Harry's relationships have ended in disaster and he is left alone and miserable. Perhaps if Harry were able to learn from his art there would be some potential for change. If Harry perhaps listened to the advice that his fictional alter ego gives him in the run-down amusement park, or if he could only listen to the advice of the devil from his latest project . . . but the only glimpse we get of any change in Harry comes toward the end of the film.

When Harry tells the college welcoming committee about his latest project, he finishes the story he began at gunpoint on the roof of his apartment complex. When he told the story to Lucy he told it in third person, starring young Harvey Stern. But this time, when one of the committee asks who the main character is Harry finally admits, "It's me, thinly disguised. In fact, I don't even think I should disguise it anymore, you know. It's me." This is an important moment in the film, in that it is the first instance where Harry, the artist, admits that he in fact is the subject of his fiction—that the art is the reality. This confession is important in that it offers the hope that Harry will one day be able to learn from his art. It is only after this honest admission that Harry is able to overcome his mental block and write again.

This confession is significant not only to Harry as a character—a character who until this moment is unable to make a meaningful connection between his fiction and his real life—but it also raises questions about the connections between *Deconstructing Harry* and director/writer Woody Allen's personal life. Is Woody admitting here that this fiction he has created—the disjointed life of a character named Harry—is equivocal with himself? Is this movie simply a confession to the public about what the personality behind the art is experiencing? Is Allen finally admitting that the stage persona is actually the man?

It is tempting to interpret this line as a sort of confession by Allen, for, after all, the situations of Woody and Harry seem quite similar. Both Woody and Harry are celebrated writers—authoring, for the most part, comic tales, stemming largely from personal experiences. Both see a psychoanalyst on a regular basis; both are estranged fathers, and both have injured others in their licentiousness. It is as if Allen is tempting us to conflate the character and the author—to confuse the fiction with reality. And this is where we see the genius of Woody Allen. In a film that deals with the artist's inability to approach life except through art and, in the end, to even distinguish between the two—the art overwhelming his life to the extent that it becomes unclear who are the fictional characters are and who the "real" people are—Allen ingeniously tempts the audience to question the reality of the film: Is the film an elaborate confession? Is the "fictional" character of the film, as Harry admits to the doting college group, merely a "thinly disguised" stand-in for the real thing? Is the art in fact reality?

Woody Allen's films lend themselves to deconstruction. He writes, directs, and stars in almost every one of his films. He draws heavily on personal experience; he hand-picks the soundtrack and the locations. His heroes and heroines are consummate psychoanalysis patients; they are neurotic, haunted by phobias, isolated, self-conscious, usually Manhattanites, and abnormally witty. In short, they end up largely resembling the persona the public has come to know as Woody Allen. In such a case, it's hard not to analyze, to deconstruct the art to find the life behind it. For after all, what, if it is not the overwhelming individuality of his films, are we so attracted to in the work of Woody Allen? Yes, we want to understand the human psyche a little better; we want a few laughs and to enjoy a few classic jazz tunes. But when one truly considers it, it becomes clear that what is so attractive about the films of Woody Allen is the detailed examination they give us of *a* human psyche—the psyche of Woody Allen.

And that is exactly what made '92 such a de(con)structive year. The moment the scandal hit the papers (stealing the front page of *Time* and *Newsweek* out from under the Republican convention), critics and moviegoers alike began to dismantle the public works of Woody Allen in order to find the truth about his private life. But all of this was anticipated. Allen is and has been well aware of the precarious nature of his celebrity status. In a number of his films, most notably *Stardust Memories* and *Zelig*, Allen addresses some of the anxieties and consequences that stalk (sometimes literally) a celebrated figure.

Deconstructing Harry addresses these concerns in a more relevant and personal way. In what is revealed to the audience, Harry appears to enjoy a healthy public image. The college that threatened to expel him years ago, now seems to have a great deal of respect for him, going through enough trouble to stage an award ceremony and to bestow upon him an honorary degree. He is well liked in the literary world as well. As Lucy (Julia Davis) so resentfully informs us, the critics sing the praises of his, as she calls it, "literary gold," and his "inspired comic flights." To put it simply, Harry's public life is doing well. But as we have seen, the film is not concerned with his public life. Rather it is a darkly comic and ironic examination of the failed personal life of a successful artist. The period of Allen's life in which this movie was written and produced makes this study of the wrecked personal life of an artist appear to be even more intimately tied to Allen.

Although it may sound to some critics like a confessional tale, *Deconstructing Harry* is not a personal confession on the part of Woody Allen. In the December 1, 1999 issue of *USA Today,* Allen clearly answers this himself:

> I'm not my persona. I don't sit at home drinking liquor with writer's block. I don't have a bad relationship with my sister. I didn't kidnap my kid. I didn't grow up in Coney Island, and my father did not work bumper cars. But people think it's true.

This quote is talking almost solely of the Harry Block character, revealing Allen's awareness of the equivocation of himself with that character.

The film concludes with a pseudo-happy ending. After failing to give his acceptance speech at his old college because of a minor run-in with the law (merely a case of kidnapping!), Harry finally returns to his apartment. Once again he slips from reality to fiction and finds himself in front of an applauding congregation of his characters. Harry's creations praise him and in this approval he finds relative peace and virtual meaning in (the existence of himself in) art. Since he seems to discern no higher order and meaning in life, Harry is forced to look for meaning within art alone. Until he is able to fully understand the connection between his art and his life, Harry will continue to live a disjointed and solitary existence.

Woody Allen's *Deconstructing Harry* is a masterful work. It is at once disturbing, whimsical, dark, shocking, and funny; it is a complex portrait of an artist, presented in an appropriately neurotic, digressive manner. It is entertaining in all the ways audiences expect of a Woody Allen movie—creative, energetic, spontaneous, and witty. It is also profound in its ironic nature. Allen presents us with the story of a writer who is unable to function outside of his own fiction and then tempts us to equate this character with himself. Allen tempts us to deconstruct Harry ourselves, and, in so doing, question the dubious dividing line between art and reality.

Works Cited

Bjorkman, Stig and Aflabeta Borkforlag. *Woody Allen on Woody Allen: in Conversation with Stig Bjorkman.* New York: Grove Press, 1993.

Blake, Richard A. *Woody Allen, Profane and Sacred.* London: The Scarecrow Press, Inc., 1995.

Curry, Renee R. *Perspectives on Woody Allen.* New York: G. K. Hall & Co., 1996

Fox, Julian. *Woody: Movies from Manhattan.* Woodstock, New York: The Overlook Press, 1996.

Girgus, Sam B. *The Films of Woody Allen.* Cambridge: Cambridge University Press, 1993.

Sunshine, Linda. *The Illustrated Woody Allen Reader.* New York: Alfred A. Knopf, 1993.

Woody Allen and American Character in *Deconstructing Harry*

SAM GIRGUS

The great comedic films of Woody Allen have been explorations of moral consciousness. For about a quarter century, Allen's cinematic aesthetic achieved special genius by relating the originality and exuberance of his humor to moral and cultural issues. Many have compared the social and moral dimensions of his comedic brilliance in film to Mark Twain's contribution to American humor and American literary realism. Like Twain, Allen melds aesthetic complexity with popular culture. From his films of the late 1960s and early 1970s to *Annie Hall* (1977) and on to *Crimes and Misdemeanors* (1989), Allen developed visual and verbal comedy to consider the permanence of love and identity, the meaning of a moral life in the modern world, and the relevance of values and ideals for a society without God.

Deconstructing Harry (1997) revisits the events, actions, and words of Allen's previous films to dramatize the tensions of modern nihilism upon moral consciousness. He repeats the gestures and body language of other Allen heroes such as Ike in *Manhattan* (1979); he replays the love-hatred of the sisters in *Hannah and Her Sisters* (1986); he reuses camera and mise-en-scene to review the past and place history in the present;' he reengages questions of Jewish identity as a prism for viewing life; he repeats the solipsistic egoism of alternating between the veneration and vilification of women. The results of Allen's cinematic reconstruction of these experiences epitomize the crippled moral sensibilities of our time. In this film, nihilism and hopelessness triumph. The moral dimension dissipates into stale jokes. A journey to hell in the film only inspires more exhausted jokes that counter the concept of moral accountability.

However, the strategy of making comedy out of moral desperation and psychic hollowness fails. Like a horror-film monster hiding in the ocean's depths, the semiotic genius of film rises above the surface of the director's program of self-justification. The film devours its creator in the guise of the director's own face. The power of visual representation as one of the basic semiotic elements of film undermines Allen's effort to achieve exculpation through his challenge to the reality of moral authority and boundaries. Old jokes, painfully predictable timing, and compulsive repetition fail to contain or counter the moral suggestiveness of Allen's ravaged face. Allen plays Harry Block, the sexually hyperactive antihero. Allen's face testifies not only to the inappropriateness of the film's romantic portrait of him as the lover of an array of beautiful and vibrant women. His tired visage also demonstrates the psychic damage of an ideology of moral relativism that attempts to separate actions from their consequences. Like the face of Dorian Gray, it exhibits the costs of secret evils, costs that contradict the putative harmlessness of the film's best joke about an old man's dark past. The message on Allen's aging face recalls Gloria Swanson's mask of decadence and despair in *Sunset Boulevard*, dramatizing the withering of his artistic imagination and the putrescence of his moral energy.

In previous Allen films such as *Crimes and Misdemeanors*, Jewishness and Judaism structure his engagement with real and profound issues of morality and identity. In Harry's world, however, the derivative treatment of religion echoes Allen's exhaustion. Even the film's greatest success, its structuration of a complex self-reflexive narrative form, self-consciously reenacts Philip Roth's themes of Jewish alienation and the tension between art and reality. Although Allen brilliantly interweaves scenes of Harry's perception of real life and characters with his fictional rendition of them, the film's exploitation of classic Roth material suggests the enervation of Allen's powers of invention and the attenuation of his capacity to mature. In the film, Stanley Tucci resembles Roth, while Richard Benjamin reminds us of his role in the film version of "Good-bye, Columbus." In the same year as the appearance of *Deconstructing Harry*, Roth proffers a coherent view of the degeneration of the American myth in *American Pastoral*, and Norman Mailer imagines and maintains a consistent voice and vision of a radical Jesus in *The Gospel According to the Son*. Compared to these literary works by figures of Allen's generation and cultural milieu, Allen in his film contrives a self-pitying vision of the total power of blackness and nothingness in shaping human destiny. This trite and reductionist response to evil and uncertainty becomes a case for justifying personal delinquency and tolerating moral and psychological chaos.

The moral nihilism and artistic redundancy of *Deconstructing Harry* help explain Maureen Dowd's reaction to the film as "a kind of iceberg—make that a Konigsberg" when she went to see it on "a rainy afternoon." She found the movie to be more damaging to people than Titanic so that she could not "stop thinking" about certain "perfectly obvious" issues. "It's concluding argument is that art extenuates morality, that ordinary ethical standards do not apply to people who produce extraordinary art" (33).

Beyond the film's fallacious argument about the immunity of art from moral responsibility, the notion persists in the film of morality as another human invention or fiction. At one time such ideas constituted for Allen an existential and moral challenge to examine and structure experience. However, while creating these days under the influence of deconstruction, Allen ends this film where *Manhattan* begins—with a voice-over of a writer finding his language. In *Manhattan*, the voice-over prefaces a landmark film. In *Deconstructing Harry*, the voice-over anticipates more bad jokes; life, art, thought, and love are reduced to the sex act that seems to define and obsess our time.

Works Cited

Dowd, Maureen. "Sex and Self-Pity." *Liberties*. Nov. 29, 1998, 31–35.
Mailer, Norman. *The Gospel According to the Son*. New York: Random House, 1997.
Roth, Philip. *American Pastoral*. Boston: Houghton Mifflin, 1997.

Deconstructing *Everyone Says I Love You* and *Sweet and Lowdown*

KIMBALL KING

The last five years of the twentieth century were extremely productive ones for Woody Allen. As writer, director and/or actor, he contributed to *Bullets Over Broadway* (1995), *Central Park West* (1995), *Everyone Says I Love You* (1995), *Mighty Aphrodite* (1996), *Deconstructing Harry* (1997), *Celebrity* (1998) and *Sweet and Low Down* (1999), as well as continuing work on television productions.

Allen has always been iconoclastic and original, but there is a conspicuous modernity to his most recent works which appear to dissect not only his own life (as in *Deconstructing Harry* or *Celebrity*) but respected film genres, such as the American musical in *Everyone Says I Love You* and the documentary-style biography one associates with Public Television in *Sweet and Lowdown*. These latter two works are united by their strong dependence on sustained musical interludes, although the music, in *Everyone Says* bears the stamp of the ASCAP (American Society of Composers, Authors, and Publishers) Broadway show, whereas the guitar-playing in *Sweet and Lowdown* explores the jazz tradition with its roots in both African-American culture and an alienated, sometimes mournful departure from mainstream cheerfulness. While there are points of comparison in the two films, the 1995 movie focuses on the affluent, with lavish settings in New York, Venice, and Paris, and Allen's more recent film captures ordinary people in slightly tawdry boardwalk settings and dimly lit nightclubs in poorer neighborhoods. Yet each work challenges a cultural genre in hilariously disruptive ways. Beginning with *Everyone Says I Love You*, one notices in the opening shot the unex-

pected surprise of nonsingers performing a traditional love song, Ray-
mond Klages and Jesse Greer's "Just You, Just Me." The result is infec-
tiously appealing but it also warns the viewer that expected musical
"conventions" will be challenged, with both touching and comic results.
An awareness of the relationship of popular music to larger culture is not
new to Allen. Like playwright Tom Stoppard, whose protagonist in the
recently revived *The Real Thing*, speaks eloquently of the powerful emotional impact of "pop" tunes, Allen's background music in all of his
films, mentioned in detail in numerous articles in this collection, has had
a significant influence on the tone of his works. In particular he appreciates the amateur rendition of a musical piece that may be deeply affect-
ing at the same time it is amusingly inept. Diane Wiest's failed singing
audition in *Hannah and Her Sisters* (1986) comes to mind. Audience
laughter signifies an awareness that as a professional performer she is
"doomed"; and yet she reveals for the first time in the film that she is a
deeply sympathetic person, and she captured the soulful essence of a
song often made sterile by more accomplished vocalists. In the justly famous American musical tradition, beautiful looking performers with ex-
ceptional voices and graceful bodies rendered precise, ideal musical
show-stoppers, which could, of course, never be sung or danced as com-
petently by ordinary people. Nevertheless, audiences were lured into
singing or humming the same tunes, partly in an attempt to capture the
gaiety and optimism of the theatrical production. Similarly complicated
production numbers were impressively choreographed so that masses of
chorus girls and boys formed a flawless background of swaying movement for master dancers, people like Astaire and Rogers or Kelly and
Hayworth, who took center stage. The principal lovers in each musical
never grew old and their frequently inappropriate outbursts of song, such
as a moonstruck Lothario singing on his beloved's doorstep or an office
full of clerks and secretaries dancing on desk tops when the boss went to
the water cooler, were accepted by audiences as conditions of a respected
artistic genre. Then, too, every successful musical in the Broadway stage
or on Hollywood's screens boasted original musical numbers which
often became independently popular.

Allen tweaks all of these show business staples in *Everyone Says I
Love You*. Most importantly his principle actors, while they may have
pleasant voices, are nonsingers. Ed Norton and Drew Barrymore, appearing first as if they are romantic leads make it very apparent that they
possess little native talent in the film's opening musical number, a revival
of an old ASCAP song, "Just You, Just Me." Norton, pleasant-looking

but not handsome, sings in a flat, softly off-key voice. Yet the effect is not unappealing. Soon countless New Yorkers join in with additional voices of the song as they go about their daily rounds. The mixture of professionals and nonprofessionals in the movie serves to underscore Allen's spoof of conventions. When Norton selects an engagement ring at Harry Winston's, he croons "My Baby Just Cares For Me," another classic Broadway tune. Here not only his faltering voice but his awkward gestures are mocked as he dances clumsily on table tops at the exclusive jeweler's while professional dancers execute a beautifully choreographed number in a tiny space. The choice of Harry Winston as jeweler was serendipitous. Rumor has it that Allen first approached Tiffany and Company for staging this scene but the store would not agree to alleged Tiffany salesmen dancing on jewelry counters. The Winston firm, far more daunting and exclusive as an institution catering to the rich became an especially improbable venue for horseplay, and this was underscored in Allen's final list of screen credits, where he thanked "The Harry Winston Players." A hospital scene where nurses, doctors, and bandaged patients dance in the corridors to Gus Kahand and Walter Donaldson's "Making Whoopee" further advances Allen's satire on the "Good Ole Days" musical tradition. Similarly, another nonsinger with a soothing voice, actor Tim Roth, becomes improbably romantic when he woos Drew Barrymore with "If I Had You." Nevertheless, the show's most exaggerated departure from classical musicals of the stage or screen occurs when Allen himself and Goldie Hawn, playing his former wife, sing "I'm Through with Love" and dance in evening clothes alongside the Seine in Paris. Allen's gestures are predictably stiff and graceless. Hawn is literally lifted high above him in the air and appears to be flying through the sky at certain moments. Yet, incredibly, the scene provides one of the film's most touching moments. A middle-aged couple who can barely sing, and who only dance with the aid of cinematic gimmickry manage to project a sense of mutual caring and an acceptance of past romantic failures that is tender rather than absurd. At the conclusion of this spectacle, the camera cuts to the face of a stone-faced *gendarme* who has supposedly watched the entire scene. As he walks away silently, the audience is amused by their imagining what he must be thinking. Thus, Allen has anticipated any critic who would doubt the sincerity of the Allen-Hawn performance. In most musicals the concluding song-and-dance number confirms a budding romance rather than serving as an elegy for one that vanished years before. The faces of older people guessing what their lives might have been would never have been shown. Virtually every convention of musical theatre is violated *in Everybody Says I Love You*, but the lure of songs with memorable lyrics and hummable tunes and romantic stories which promise happy endings to good-hearted people is preserved. In deconstructing the musical, Allen has rescued it from historical oblivion and exposed its fundamental, enduring appeal.

Everybody Says I Love You creates nostalgia in audiences who recognize the anachronisms and the presently unacceptable artifice of musical dramas. *Sweet and Lowdown* appeals to the contemporary theater critic familiar with VH1's "Behind the Music" superstar exposés, one who appreciates the "truthfulness" of the documentary format and who enjoys sifting through a collage of contradictory viewpoints on the nature of talent and biographical accuracy. Allen presents a faux documentary of Emmet Ray, a jazz guitarist who probably never existed, and "authenticates" his existence by "interviewing" famous actors and musicians who claim to have known the mysterious star. Again, Allen scrutinizes the popular docudrama format and reveals its essential phoniness. At the same time he acknowledges the appeal of a medium which will not gloss over the foibles of its most talented people and which tries to present art and life unsentimentally. Like the musicals of Rogers and Hammerstein or Cole Porter, however, the newer docudramas are better at expressing yearnings than truths. The central means by which Allen deconstructs this newer form of entertainment is by juxtaposing a genuine jazz guitarist with his apocryphal one—in this instance the famous European gypsy, Django Reinhardt, with the fictional Emmet. The two are linked imaginatively when Allen creates a special neurosis for Emmet, a kind of "Reinhardt phobia," (Supposedly, Emmet fainted the one time he met the gypsy guitarist and he refers to him obsessively in his conversations). Our inability to understand the "real" guitarist or to appraise the nature of his musical genius is underscored by Allen's ability to conjure up a fictional musician of similar gifts.

For the film Allen persuaded well known people to play themselves and to act as documentary "experts" on the life of the fictitious Emmet Ray. Nat Hentoff, Douglas McGrath, and Ben Thomson all play themselves and relate various anecdotes about Ray, sometimes claiming that events were "alleged" or, at least subject to verification, and at other times presenting material as factual. Woody Allen also plays himself, but as the master conjurer, he soon reveals himself to be the ultimate unreliable narrator. Thus, a series of narrators are, in fact, co-conspirators, creating the myth of a guitarist who exists only in the author/director's imagination. And there are other formulaic patterns to Emmet's biography. An unhappy childhood prepared the foundations of adult neurosis. Supposedly he was raised in a brothel, where he learned to distrust and to make use of all women. He never matures into an independent person and frequently finds solace in binge drinking. The musician's love life parallels the complexities of relationships involving real-life entertainers. Emmet, brilliantly portrayed by the sullen Sean Penn, is torn between a good woman, Hattie, played by Samantha Mortin, and a bad one, Blanche, played by Uma Thurman. Emmet is primarily attracted to Hattie because she is physically mute and because she accepts him totally as he is—egotistical, unreliable, obsessed with watching trains go by and with shooting rats in an abandoned quarry. Allen and other narrators suggest that Emmet abandons Hattie out of jealousy, because she is discovered by Hollywood talent scouts and becomes a famous star of silent movies. The fact that the audience is shown clips of Hattie's movies appears to authenticate her existence and stardom. Yet the face of the woman in the silent films, while she superficially appears similar to Hattie is, in fact, a little known British film actress who actually lived and worked in Hollywood. One wonders, of course, what Allen may be saying about the need for a genius to have a noncompetitive partner. In any event the more glamorous Blanche who is a "socialite" becomes Emmet's choice for a wife, although she soon becomes unfaithful to him with a gangster.

Allen provides several directorial "signatures" that attest to his own imagination rather than to the fabricated attributes of his conjured-up guitarist. He adds a level of slapstick when he "reveals" that Emmet designed a mechanical moon to be lowered onto a stage as part of his swashbuckling nightclub entrance. But Emmet behaves like the timid Woody Allen character of the writer's earlier films and after his baseless fear of failure has tormented him for hours prior to his performance, he, indeed, manages to shift about so awkwardly that his beautiful, moon-chair device becomes unhinged and he collapses ignominiously on the stage floor. Similarly, the director/writer's fascination with gangsters leads to a Keystone cop-type car chase—a favorite event in period films, especially comedies, and one destined to challenge the credibility of Emmet's behavior. The 1930's wardrobes of the actors, the large, classic automobiles and the yellow-toned stylized cinematography of *Sweet and Lowdown* seem to celebrate a half century or more of romantic films about talented artists who were doomed to sacrifice personal fulfillment as they attempted to satisfy the demands of their selfish audiences. Rather than ending his film with a tragically disappointed and largely forgotten star of an earlier era, Allen merely causes Emmet to disappear. Neither tragedy nor eventual happiness will mark the final years of Emmet Ray. Like a magician with a wand, Allen banishes Emmet to nonexistence; the artist in control is clearly the *auteur* film director who prints the final verdict in his "biographical" subject.

Both *Everyone Says I Love You* and *Sweet and Low*down reveal a newly confident Woody Allen, an artist who has ultimate power over other artists and who can demonstrate that the public's need for icons and particular cultural venues can be both explained and manipulated by a master cinematic craftsman.

Conversations with Woody

ERIC LAX

For nearly thirty years I've had the pleasure of watching an artist's evolution from close range but I wouldn't have laid money on the chances of that after our first meeting. In the spring of 1971 an editor at *The New York Times* magazine—which was then famous for commissioning many more articles than it used—sent me off to investigate three ideas for a possible story. One of them was a profile of Woody Allen, who had just finished *Bananas* and was making the transition from stand-up comedian to filmmaker. I telephoned his managers Jack Rollins and Charles Joffe to ask for an interview and an appointment was made. I arrived at the Rollins and Joffe duplex office on West 57th Street with a couple of pages of questions and a brand new tape recorder and was taken upstairs where Woody was waiting in a small room furnished with a couple of nicely stuffed chairs. He looked uncomfortable and seemed shy. We shook hands, said hello, settled into the seats and I, rather nervously, asked my questions. His answers were succinct. His shortest was "No," which would not have been so bad if his longest had not been "Yes."

So I wrote a piece on one of the other two ideas I looked into (true to form, *The Times* didn't run it) and figured I was done with Woody Allen.

Six months later, while riding a bicycle in Sausalito, California, I was nearly run down by a Ford station wagon with a card in the front window that read, "Rollins and Joffe Productions." In that day's *Chronicle* I had seen a short article about Woody being in San Francisco to film *Play It Again, Sam* (1972) and, being young and solipsistic and without a sense of logic, I figured that instead of mere coincidence, maybe this was a sign that he was ready to talk more openly. I called Charlie Joffe to see about another interview and was summoned to a houseboat, which Woody was considering for a scene in the film. We chatted about baseball and a couple of other things and then he excused himself to look at something with the location manager. A few minutes later, Charlie came over and said, "Why don't you come on the set and hang around but be sure to keep quiet and out of the way, otherwise you'll have to go."

I dutifully did as I was told and after a few days Woody came over between shots and we talked for a minute. He came back later and we talked longer. Soon we began more formal interviews. *The Times* commissioned a profile and I stayed through much of the filming. As Woody didn't direct *Sam*, my editor suggested I also interview him while he acted in and directed *Everything You Always Wanted to Know About Sex* (1972). I Went to Los Angeles, talked with him at more length, and turned in my story the day *Time* ran a cover story on Woody.

In journalism as in comedy, timing is everything. After *The Times* killed my piece, I sent it to Woody with a note thanking him for his time and saying that at least he should see the results of all the hours he spent with me. I didn't particularly expect to hear from him but a couple of days later he called to say that he was sorry the piece wouldn't run.

"You quoted me accurately in context, and you honored my jokes," he added, meaning that I had not used a punch line without setting it up. "Feel free to stop by my editing room whenever you like."

Some weeks later I did and we've been talking ever since; our conversations have turned into what may be the oldest established permanent floating interview in New York. We talk on film sets and in his editing room, in dressing room trailers and cars, and more often than not, in the living room of his penthouse apartment with a sweeping view of Manhattan. From 1971 until 1999, when he sold it and bought a large house a mile up the avenue, we sat in the same two chairs about three feet from each other. In new surroundings, we have stayed with old ways. It is almost a ritual. He first offers me a drink; I ask for a glass of water. We have a few minutes of social conversation and bits of catch-up, then settle down to work. I put a tape recorder on an arm of his chair and we chat for an hour or two. No longer one word, his answers to my questions come in well-ordered paragraphs—thoughtful, candid, often witty, and sometimes hilarious, though I've never heard him trying to be funny. Occasionally he stops to answer the phone, then picks up where he left off.

Woody Allen is the antithesis of his screen character, who is usually frantic and in crisis. He is in control of his work and his time. His self-assessment is apt: "I'm a serious person, a disciplined worker, interested in writing, interested in literature, interested in theater and film. I'm not so inept as I depict myself for comic purposes. I know my life is not a series of catastrophic problems that are funny because they are so ludicrous. It's a much duller existence."

Decades of success and fame have made him more comfortable and less shy in general, and our meetings are genial and at ease. When I was researching the first edition of *Woody Allen* (Da Capo Press is republishing it in the fall of 2000, with an additional chapter that covers the past ten years), I decided the time to stop interviewing him would be when he started to tell me the same stories. It was three years before he repeated himself; by then I was a year past my original deadline. One day while the book was being edited, he called.

"I've been thinking about something we recently talked about and I have some more ideas, if they'd be of any interest to you," he said.

"Sorry," I told him. "You had your chance."

Or not.

Selected Bibliography

Allen, Woody. *Woody Allen on Woody Allen*. Ed. Stig Bjorkman. New York: Grove, 1995.

———. "Film Clip: Woody Allen." Interview by Roger Ebert. *The Woody Allen Companion*. 55–59. Ed. Stephen J. Spignesi. Kansas City: Andrews and McMeel, 1992. First published in *Roger Ebert's Movie Home Companion*.

Benayoun, Robert. *The Films of Woody Allen*. New York: Harmony Books, 1986.

Blake, Richard A. *Woody Allen: Profane and Sacred*. London: The Scarecrow Press, 1995.

Brode, Douglas. *The Films of Woody Allen: Revised and Updated*. Secaucus, New Jersey: Citadel Press, 1991.

Curry, Renee R. *Perspectives on Woody Allen*. New York: G. K. Hall & Co., 1996.

"Deconstructing Woody: A Critical Symposium on Woody Allen's *Deconstructing Harry*." *Cineaste*, Summer 1998.

"Deconstructomg Woody: A Critical Symposium on Woody Allen's *Deconstructing Harry*." *Cineaste*, Summer 1998.

Fox, Julian. *Woody: Movies from Manhattan*. Woodstock, New York: The Overlook Press, 1996.

Girgus, Sam B. *The Films of Woody Allen*. New York: Cambridge University Press, 1993.

Gittleson, Natalie. "The Maturing of Woody Allen." *The New York Times Magazine*, April 22, 1979.

Hirsch, Foster. *Love, Sex, Death and the Meaning of Life: The Films of Woody Allen.* New York: Limelight Editions, 1990.

Hirschberg, Lynn. "Woody Allen, Martin Scorcese." *The New York Times Magazine,* November 16, 1997.

Jacobs, Diane. *. . . but we need the eggs: The Magic of Woody Allen.* New York: St. Martin's Press, 1982.

Lax, Eric. *On Being Funny: Woody Allen and Comedy.* New York: Charterhouse, 1975.

———. *Woody Allen: A Biography.* New York: Knopf, 1991.

Lee, Sander H. *Woody Allen's Angst.* Jefferson, NC: McFarland, 1997.

McCann, Graham. *Woody Allen: New Yorker.* 1990. Cambridge, UK: Polity, 1991.

Nichols, Mary P. *Reconstructing Woody: Art, Love, and Life in the Films of Woody Allen.* Lanham, MD: Rowman & Littlefield, 1998.

O'Connor, John J. "TV Weekend: Woody Allen Revisits a Venue of Long Ago." *New York Times*, 16 Dec. 1994, D22.

Pogel, Nancy. *Woody Allen.* Boston: Twayne, 1987.

Wernblad, Annette. *Brooklyn Is Not Expanding: Woody Allen's Comic Universe.* Rutherford, NJ: Farleigh Dickinson University Press, 1992.

Yarcowar, Maurice. *Loser Take All: The Comic Art of Woody Allen.* New York: Frederick Ungar, 1979.